THE POWER
OF THE
PLATFORM

SPEAKERS ON SUCCESS

www.LVCSB.com
Las Vegas Convention Speakers Bureau

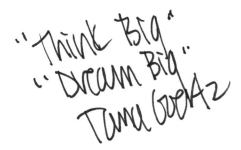

"Think Big"
"Dream Big"
Tana Goertz

THE POWER OF THE PLATFORM
Speakers on Success

Published by TwoBirds Publishing, Inc.
and
Las Vegas Convention Speakers Bureau
www.LVCSB.com

2657 Windmill Pkwy, #116, Henderson, NV 89074

Copyright © 2009 TwoBirds Publishing, Inc.
Library of Congress Control Number: 2008908985
ISBN-10: 0-975-45815-9
ISBN-13: 978-0-975-45815-0

Cover Design by Julia Lauer with Ambush Graphics
Editing and Composition by Robin Jay,
Judy Colbert, & Michelle Littleton
Formatted by Randi Ball with Obsessive Formatting &
Design

Special Note: This edition of "The Power of the Platform - Speakers on Success" is designed to provide information and motivation to our readers. It is sold with the understanding, that the publisher is not engaged to render any type of psychological, legal, or any other kind of professional advice. The content of each article is the sole expression and opinion of its author, and not necessarily that of the publisher. No warranties or guarantees are expressed or implied by the publisher's choice to include any of the content in this volume. Neither the publisher nor the individual author(s) shall be liable for any physical, psychological, emotional, financial, or commercial damages, including but not limited to special, incidental, consequential or other damages. Our view and rights are the same: You are responsible for your own choices, actions, and results.

Printed in the United States of America

ACKNOWLEDGEMENTS
Robin Jay

Special thanks to my father, **Dr. Erwin Jay**, who always held motivational speakers in high esteem; I couldn't help but aspire to be one.

Thanks, too, to each of my incredible coauthors. Your contributions are outstanding, and because of the care you put forth in crafting the perfect messages, I know that this book will help everyone who is fortunate enough to read it.

Betty LeDoux-Morris heard me speak and e-mailed me to follow up; we've been friends ever since. I treasure my old friends but I've always got room in my heart for new friends – especially when they are as genuine and supportive as Betty.

And thanks to my dear friends - neighbors, former co-workers, and associates – who support me no matter what I do or where I go.

I also want to thank my cousins, **Debbie Smith** and **Jodi Manfredi.** Talk about a support team! We grew up together and are still such close friends; I love them dearly. I also want to thank my mother, **Love**, for her unyielding support.

Special thanks to my dear friend **Judy Colbert**. Judy helped me to edit this book. Her insights, experience, and talent are evident throughout. It was my goal to make this book as comprehensive and cohesive as possible. Judy acheived that by not just editing for grammar, but also for thought. If a passage didn't come across just so or something needed was missing, Judy caught it and fixed it.

And, unless we prefer to take the hard road, we need mentors to help us on our journey. My heartfelt thanks go to my mentor, **Don Boyer**. Mentorship can be sharing experiences and insights, how-to instruction or simply encouragement. Aside from all of this, which Don shared enthusiastically, I have to thank him for the "thunk on the head." It was *just* what I needed! You and **Melinda** rock.

FOREWORD

On December 6, 2007 at the Landmark Theater in Los Angeles, California, I stood facing a crowd of 300 people. Standing next to me were Bob Proctor, Vic Johnson, Marie Diamond, Tony Alessandra, and Paul Martinelli. The crowd of friends and colleagues were there to view the premiere of our personal development film, The Power of Mentorship. The entire event took my breath away; it was one of the most amazing experiences of my life.

As of this printing, I have created and published 15 editions of The Power of Mentorship series of books - selling more than 115,000 copies worldwide. And there I was, hosting a premiere at the Landmark Theater. I look back and ask myself how in the world did I ever come upon such good fortune? The resounding answer that keeps coming back is "Professional Speakers."

I share the above accomplishments with you not to boast by any means, but to convey to you the important role professional speakers can play in your overall success in life.

I owe all of my good fortune to the professional speakers who have imparted their knowledge, insights and wisdom into my life over the past 25 years. I gained their mentorship through their books, courses and, most of all, from their presentations from the platform. I will forever be grateful for the influence and education that professional speakers have had in my life.

This is one reason I was so excited and honored to be asked to write the foreword for this outstanding book, "The Power of the Platform."

Robin Jay has done a remarkable job compiling the writings of some of the most powerful and effective professional platform speakers of the 21st Century. These featured speakers have spoken to millions of people across the globe, making a positive impact in their lives, bringing information, inspiration and motivation.

Now, you too can benefit from the wisdom and experience of these speakers. Every chapter carries its own unique message, insight, and wisdom. I encourage you to read every chapter carefully, take extensive notes and put into action the laws of success you glean from each writer.

I know of no one better suited to compile an anthology of speakers than Robin Jay. She is an accomplished author and speaker whose energy and enthusiasm is downright contagious both on and off the platform. As President of the Las Vegas Convention Speakers Bureau, she is well qualified to hand-pick each contributing author/speaker ensuring you, the reader, a fabulous and informative read.

The Power of the Platform condenses hours of teaching and years of experience into an easy-to-read book. Without the power of good books and the life-changing messages of professional speakers, I am sure my life would have taken a far different course.

Whether you are looking for a quick read that delivers inspiration and motivation or an in-depth business idea and concept, you will find it here in this marvelous anthology.

Remember, as my mentor told me many years ago, "Who you listen to determines what you get, where you go, and where you end up." Every one of these contributing authors is speaking to you. Listen well my friend because they can help you reach your grandest dreams.

Don Boyer

Creator of the hit movie
The Power of Mentorship-The Movie

www.ThePowerOfMentorship.com

TABLE OF CONTENTS

Introduction 7

Chapter One - Success Begins with Believing
Jack Canfield 10

Chapter Two - Taming the Alligators in Your Life
Dr. Nick Hall 16

Chapter Three - A Grain of Sand
Charli Douglass 24

Chapter Four - Blogging Your Way to Business Success
Andy Ebon 32

Chapter Five - The Joy of Change
Amanda Gore 42

Chapter Six - Think Like a Champion
Jim Fannin 48

Chapter Seven - I Was Born to Sell; What Were You Born to Do?
Tana Goertz 56

Chapter Eight - When Things Go Wrong, Don't Go With Them!
Les Brown 64

Chapter Nine - Fat on Success
Angelique Daniels 70

Chapter Ten - Being the Best
Tony Alessandra 78

Chapter Eleven - Stormie's Communication Nation
Stormie Andrews 86

Chapter Twelve - F.A.I.L.U.R.E. is NOT a Four-Letter Word!
Karl Schilling 94

Chapter Thirteen - Passion + Purpose = Success
Dr. Caroline Williams 102

Chapter Fourteen - My Pivotal Moment
Michelle Littleton..110

Chapter Fifteen - Step Up and Step Into Leadership
Yasmine Bijan 118

Chapter Sixteen - Discovering Your Soul's Purpose
Dale Halaway 126

Chapter Seventeen - Discipline: The Key to Success
Judi Moreo 134

Chapter Eighteen - Six Serious Fear Busters
Marcia Wieder 138

Chapter Nineteen - Are You a Superhero?
Johnny Murillo...146

Chapter Twenty - The Uncertainty Principle
Brian Tracy 154

Chapter Twenty-One - Life's a Gamble
Marion Grobb Finkelstein 160

INTRODUCTION

Congratulations! You are in possession of a book that will change your life. The messages herein are positively *transformational!*

Growing up, my father would discipline me and my sister Terri by making us sit in front of the big, console hi-fi stereo to listen to Earl Nightingale's masterpiece, *Lead the Field.* Earl has been called "The Father of Personal Development." Dad said that hearing Earl speak "live" and later listening to his audio programs literally changed his life. We learned early on that "Good attitude equals good results; bad attitude equals bad results." Good or bad - the mind does not care; it simply responds to our attention... as does the universe.

My father set an incredible example for us, as well as for my brother, Barry, and my step-brother, James. Dad is huge fan of personal development. Whenever there is a book I want to read, I call my father first to see if it's already in what I call "Dr. Jay's Library," and if he'll pass it along to me.

My father implemented everything he learned. He built a veritable optometric empire of offices throughout the Greater Cleveland area in the days before national eyewear chains. In retrospect, I have to admit that my father had found a positive, constructive method for teaching us how to become successful and happy. After all, parents don't always have the right answers themselves! These lessons must have sunk in, because I find myself enjoying a career as an award-winning author, motivational speaker and now, as a publisher. As enlightened adults, we continue our quest for knowledge, understanding and inspiration.

Several years ago, I decided to launch the Las Vegas Convention Speakers Bureau (*www. LVCSB.com*). Though it started as a humble venture, it has grown as I've surrounded myself with some of the most incredible speakers in the industry. I live in the #1 meeting capital of the world, Las Vegas, which is host to some of the biggest and best conventions. It's a match made in heaven.

This book is the icing on the cake. Deciding to publish an anthology that would feature messages from some of the best speakers in the business made perfect sense. Now, people everywhere can get the same shot of inspiration as they would when hearing a keynote address... anytime, in the convenience of a paperback.

As each coauthor contributed to this anthology, I became increasingly impressed by the content of their messages. There is not a chapter in this book that can't change your life for the better, help you in business, or improve your relationships. It is positively *divine!* I knew that bringing together some of the finest motivational speakers in one book to share their various messages would be a great idea. But as I edited this book, I found myself forwarding a chapter here and there to various friends or relatives who needed *exactly* that message at that time. I believe that you will connect with the writings in this book in such a profound way as to be positively transformed.

I am so excited to present this anthology to you. The coauthors are some of the most respected and caring individuals in the industry. Don't be surprised when, as you read each chapter, you think to yourself, "I believe this speaker wrote this message just for me! It's *exactly* what I needed to know right now."

With love and positive thoughts,

Robin Jay

As the beloved originator of the **Chicken Soup for the Soul**® series, **Jack Canfield** watched the series grow to a billion dollar market. This alone makes him uniquely qualified to talk about success. He is also the author of the best-selling *The Success Principles: How to Get from Where You Are to Where You Want to Be.*

Affectionately known as "America's #1 Success Coach," Jack is America's leading expert in creating peak performance for entrepreneurs, leaders, managers, sales professionals, employees and educators. Over the past 30 years he's helped hundreds of thousands of individuals achieve their dreams.

Jack is a Harvard graduate with a Master's Degree in psychological education and is one of the earliest champions of peak performance. He has a gift for sharing his methodology and results-oriented activities to help others produce breakthrough results. Visit his website *www. JackCanfield.com* for more information on booking him for your next event.

Chapter One

Success Begins with Believing

Jack Canfield

I have written constantly about how in order to be successful, we must first define what success means to us, and that means getting CLEAR about what you want, writing it down, and thinking BIG!

If you are going to be *successful* in creating the life of your dreams, you also have to believe that you are capable of making it happen.

You have to believe you have the right stuff, that you are able to pull it off. You have to believe in yourself.

Whether you call it self-esteem, self-confidence, or self-assurance, it is a deep-seated belief that you have what it takes – the abilities, inner resources, talents, and skills to create your desired results.

Ultimately, you must learn to control your self-talk, eliminate any negative and limiting beliefs, and maintain a constant state of positive expectations.

Control Your Self-Talk
Researchers have found that the average person thinks as many as 50,000 thoughts a day. Sadly, many of those thoughts are negative — I'm not management material... I'll never lose weight... It doesn't matter what I do, nothing ever works out for me. This is what psychologists call victim language.

Victim language actually keeps you in a victim state of mind. It is a form of self-hypnosis that lulls you into a belief that you are unlovable and incompetent.

In order to get what you want from life, you need to give up this victim language and start talking to yourself like a winner — "I can do it"... "I know there is a solution"... "I am smart enough and strong enough to figure this out"... "Everything I eat helps me maintain my perfect body weight."

You Are Always Programming Your Subconscious Mind
Your subconscious mind is like the crew of a ship. You are it's captain. It is your job to give the crew orders. And when you do this, the crew takes everything you say literally.

The crew (your subconscious) has no sense of humor. It just blindly follows orders.

When you say, "Everything I eat goes straight to my hips," the crew hears that as an order: "Take everything she eats, turn it into fat and put it on her hips."

On the other hand, if you say, "Everything I eat helps me maintain my perfect body weight," the crew will begin to make that into reality by helping you make better food choices, exercise, and maintain the right metabolism rate for your body.

This power of your subconscious mind is the reason you must become very vigilant and pay careful attention to your spoken and internal statements.

Unfortunately, most people don't realize they are committing negative self-talk, which is why it is best to enlist another person — your success partner — in monitoring each other's speaking. You can have a signal for interrupting each other when you use victim language.

Use Affirmations to Build Self-Confidence
One of the most powerful tools for building worthiness and self-confidence is the repetition of positive statements until they become a natural part of the way you think.

These "affirmations" act to crowd out and replace the negative orders you have been sending your crew (your subconscious mind) all these years.

I suggest that you create a list of 10 to 20 statements that affirm your belief in your worthiness and your ability to create the life of your dreams.

Of course, what to believe is up to you, but here are some examples of affirmations that have worked for others in the past:

- I am worthy of love, joy and success.
- I am smart and make wise choices.
- I am loveable and capable.
- I create anything I want.
- I am able to solve any problem that comes my way.
- I can handle anything that life hands me.
- I have all the energy I need to do everything I want to do.
- I am attracting all the right people into my life.

Believing in Yourself is an Attitude

Believing in yourself is a choice. It's an attitude you develop over time. It's now your responsibility to take charge of your own self-concept and your beliefs.

It might help to know that the latest brain research now indicates that with enough positive self-talk and positive visualization combined with the proper training, coaching, and practice, anyone can learn to do almost anything.

You must choose to believe that you can do anything you set your mind to – anything at all – because, in fact, you can!

Dr. Nick Hall is in high demand by leading corporations and elite athletes for his unique team building and motivational programs. He is an internationally recognized psychoneuroimmunologist who has conducted pioneering research dealing with the interrelationships between emotions and health.

He is an adventurer and award-winning scientist whose discoveries have been featured on "60 Minutes," "Nova," "Nightline," and the Emmy-Award winning television series "Healing and the Mind." A former alligator wrestler, Nick also was the first person to complete the grueling Baja 1000 mile off-road race on a bicycle.

His entertaining and customized programs draw upon both his medical knowledge and unusual experiences to help people cope effectively with stress and change. Visit *www.DrNickHall.com*. Dr. Hall directs team building activities and presents motivational seminars at his Saddlebrook Resort headquarters in Tampa, Florida. Call 813-907-4830 or e-mail *nhall@saddlebrookresort.com*.

Chapter Two

Taming the Alligators in Your Life

Dr. Nick Hall

Most of us know what to do. Eat healthier. Exercise 30 minutes a day. Stop smoking. Manage money better. *Just do it.* Right? So, why don't we? The truth is that we don't believe we can. As a result, fear of failure sets in. But fear can hold you back only if you let it. By controlling fear, you can achieve any reasonable and worthwhile goal you set for yourself.

Three things will keep fear from becoming goal-threatening anxiety: *control, predictability,* and *optimism.* As long as you perceive some measure of control, even the alligators in your life can be tamed. I know because I worked my way through college by wrestling alligators at the Black Hills Reptile Gardens in South Dakota. Even though I was slighter and lighter than many of the reptiles I took on, I usually won. That's because I never let fear overwhelm me. I knew I had a great deal of control despite what things might have looked like to the spectators.

For one thing, no one forced me to accept the job. Before each show, I would choose the alligator I would fight. I learned to predict what each would do when I jumped on its back. I also knew how to maneuver the alligator so it couldn't slam me with its tail. That weapon is as dangerous as its powerful jaws. Sure, there was risk. There always is. But with practice and by being prepared, you can reduce virtually any risk. That was the advice of the famous adventurer Verlen Kruger, who once logged 28,000 miles in a single canoe trip. During an interview, I asked what he would tell a young Verlen just starting out in life. He replied, *"Be prepared."*

I belong to an organization called WaterTribe, inspired by Verlen's extraordinary accomplishments. Our races cover distances that pale in comparison to his; nevertheless, the 300 mile Everglades Challenge and 1,200 mile Ultimate Challenge are far from being leisurely excursions. By being aware of the risks, we can prepare and better control our responses. Furthermore, by training under all the conditions we may experience, we can learn to predict what is likely to happen should such conditions occur during the race. Even when we may lack control, just knowing what may happen next can enable us to endure. Throw in an optimistic attitude that even the worst conditions eventually will get better, and anxiety is kept at bay.

In the final analysis, we only ever do one of two things: approach those things that give rise to pleasure or avoid those things that cause discomfort. Fear is associated with discomfort, which prompts us to avoid. Unfortunately, that avoidance sometimes spills over and influences decisions that have nothing to do with the threat. You react by avoiding *all* change, including that which may be beneficial. The avoidance signal becomes an alarm that sounds throughout your brain. Progress towards personal and professional goals is stalled as you avoid more than just what triggered that emotion. You know what to do, but now fear keeps you from doing it. And it doesn't have to be fear of bodily harm or loss. It also can be fear of failure.

You can counter this natural tendency of the brain to stay the course when fear is present. No, don't reach for the rose-colored glasses. It's unhealthy to ignore bad things when they happen. Do acknowledge them, but not to the extent that they blind you to opportunity. Begin by taking stock of everything that's gone wrong. Write it down or talk about it. This simple act helps you shift your thoughts from brain areas governing emotions to those that mediate reason. You still may be primarily in fight/flight mode, but at least you have begun to engage those brain areas that will enable you to find a solution. Now do the opposite. Make a list of all the resources you have. Shift your focus from lost assets to those you still have.

This process turned things around for me almost instantly during the 1,200 mile Ultimate Florida Challenge. My kayak's rudder snapped in two in heavy Atlantic seas depriving me of both my foot-operated and hand-operated steering systems. The pole supporting my stabilizing outrigger broke. It was after midnight on wind-swept Boynton Beach along Florida's East Coast. Anger, triggered by these mishaps, was rapidly mixed with sadness that I would most likely be unable to finish the race. There was no way to repair the metal rudder or the stabilizing system. In addition, the boat had filled with water while negotiating the rough surf. Despite claims of their being waterproof, both my light and VHF radio were no longer functioning. I concluded that I was out of the race and began thinking about the logistics of getting back across the state to my home in Tampa. I was in avoidance mode and I wanted to withdraw to the familiar setting of home.

While pacing the beach pondering my dilemma, I verbalized these thoughts, and in so doing, I was able to hear my thoughts from a source other than from my brain's emotion center. A different type of fear emerged, which was the *fear of the regret* I would experience if I were to drop out. While fear is still an avoidance-inducing emotion, I had now reframed it in a manner that would take me toward my goal.

Just by shifting my thoughts, I became more optimistic and was able to transform fear into a formula for success.

Focusing on what I still had, I realized I could still steer with a paddle. I wouldn't need the outrigger if I stayed in the protected waters of the Intracoastal Waterway. I was able to replace the light and radio, but it was still a bad situation. Tidal influences were much more powerful along the in-shore route that was longer than following a straighter course up the Atlantic. But I was once again making progress toward my goal, and I knew that if I paddled for longer days, I would still finish within the allotted time of 28 days. I made it in 26 days and 16 hours. It is rare that there is no solution. It's simply a matter of finding it.

You can do something else. You can prevent a feeling of despair by defining success with outcomes you can directly control, instead of those you can't. If you are a salesperson, your goal should be to contact five new prospects a day rather than land a new client each week. It doesn't matter if each person hangs up on you. You can't control what another person does, so don't make your success contingent upon it. Making five calls is realistic and attainable. All it requires is for you to expend the necessary effort to pick up the phone or make a personal visit. In a month's time, you will have placed about 100 calls.

In my consulting business, the research shows that you'll get a three to five percent success rate from a marketing campaign targeting a random population of potential clients. That means six to ten additional clients per month or 30 to 60 per year. Don't confuse the signed contracts with the true success. Success was making the designated number of calls. Those signed contracts are your *reward* for that success.

I apply this process to WaterTribe challenges. On a daily basis, my goal seldom is to reach a point on the chart, and certainly not the final destination. At the start of the Ultimate Florida Challenge, the destination was 1,200 miles away. Nearly two weeks would pass before the remaining distance was less than what I had covered. Weather is the primary variable determining my rate of speed, and that's something over which I have no control. I'm not going to gamble my sense of satisfaction on natural forces. Instead, my goal always is to make forward progress for 18 hours each day. On a good day with favorable winds and tides, I may cover 60 miles. On a bad one, it may be less than 20. It doesn't matter. Oh, and stopping to make repairs counts as forward progress.

I have control over the time I spend paddling, thereby giving me control over my measure of success. The slow days are frustrating, but not to the point of being demoralizing or inducing thoughts of failure. Even during days of headwinds, I can always achieve my daily goal of paddling at least 18 hours. Those daily accomplishments make it that much easier to press on, no matter how bad conditions may be. The prospect of failure is not an issue since I have a means by which to celebrate success each and every day. Success is more than reaching a goal. Success is achieved every time you make progress. *Each day, establish a realistic and worthwhile objective that is within your control.* Then watch as you create your success.

Before you know it, you'll arrive at your destination wondering what all the fuss was about.

Charli Douglass and her husband Chris own "Fitness Transformations," offering motivational workshops and lifestyle coaching. As a Personal Transformation Expert, Charli draws from nearly thirty years of experience to help her audiences achieve complete mind and body fitness. She is also a "Psych-K" facilitator, which is the practice of transforming beliefs into reality through psychology and kinesiology.

Charli is mother to two girls and enjoys spending time with them and her granddaughter.

Her passion is helping others to achieve physical and mental success, attract financial abundance, and improve their relationships. To contact Charli, visit *www.FitTips.com*, e-mail *CharliSue@cox.net*, or call 702-375-6279.

Chapter Three

A Grain Of Sand
The Secret to Unlimited Health, Wealth, and Happiness!

Charli Douglass

Acknowledging the Power

There is a very definite power at work in the Universe. We have given this power many names. Some call it the Universal Consciousness and others call it God, Buddha, or Mohammed. What you choose to call it doesn't matter, *JUST CALL IT!* Tap in to this unlimited "Source of Power" and you *will* succeed. I did and it changed my life forever.

Less than ten years ago, my family was living in the basement of my mother's house. Financially, we had hit rock bottom. Now we live in a million dollar home, own two Mercedes cars and have money in the bank. WHAT HAPPENED??

We learned about and put to use the secrets of the Universal Laws of Success.

We had tried setting goals, voicing affirmations, and using creative visualization techniques. All of these are excellent tools, but you won't succeed using just these tools alone. The secret to manifesting your dreams is to connect with your *Universal Power* first. Then, and only then, will these other tools become effective.

To make this work, you have to truly believe in the unlimited power of your higher source. Try it now; take a minute to look around, empty your mind of all thoughts and be in the now. Feel the wind, listen to the birds, and look at the trees and clouds. Understand that your Universal Power has created all of this.

It's All About FEELING

Stand on a beach and look at the billions of grains of sand. Realize that as easily as this power can create one grain of sand, it can also allow you to draw health, wealth, and happiness into your life. Your Source has unlimited power.

How do you tap in and use this magnificent force? It is easy, fun, and empowering. All you have to do is clear your mind of all thoughts: past, present, or future. Just do the following life changing technique for 1-3 minutes, a couple of times a day:

Begin by asking yourself two questions: What time is it? The answer is always.... **NOW!**

Where are you?
The answer is always .... **HERE!**

Then ....EMPTY THE TRASH! Trash is anything that is occupying your mind... thoughts about things that HAVE happened or MIGHT happen. It is "TRASH" – so DUMP IT!

For just a few minutes... stop the self talk (your internal dialogue), and focus on what's happening around you now – at this very moment. Remember that there are no "ordinary" moments. Something is always going on!

When you are in this peaceful state, you will become aware of the wind blowing... dogs barking... birds chirping... the sounds of nearby traffic. You'll hear whatever is happening around you. There are no distractions; you're tuning in to what is happening right NOW. Enjoy it in peace and harmony. The pressure will release, and you will draw more of what you want into your life because when your mind is a complete blank, you are in contact with your Source. Being one with your Source allows you to share Its unlimited power and you will draw everything you want into your life.

After a few minutes of being in the Now with no thoughts, ask yourself this: How do you FEEL? The answer is always *AWESOME!* This is the secret that will draw all of the happiness you could ever imagine into your life.

The more times you FEEL truly happy, the more you are drawing what you want into your life. Watching your kids doing something cute, seeing your dog run and play, your spouse showing you affection... even the clouds painting a picture across the sky... All of these are gifts for you from the universe. Every time you truly experience the FEELINGS associated with these wonderful gifts, you are on your way to fulfilling your dreams.

Conversely, every time you experience fear, doubt, or uncertainty, you are closing your mind to your Source and pushing away that which what you want. PRACTICE feeling good. It will get easier to connect the more you do this. Practice smiling every minute you can, because it creates the fuel that powers the universe to give you everything you want!

In real life, this is how connecting to your Source works. I learned that whenever I let go and trust in my Universal Source, **good things happen**. I detached myself from my husband's bad habits and negativity and, over the years, I was able to turn my "frog" back into Chris, the "prince" I married.

How did I do it? I started by keeping a "Grateful Journal." Each morning, I would find one thing about him that I liked. Believe me, for the state we were in, there were days when I really had to search to find anything positive about my "frog." One day, when I was hard-pressed to find anything positive, I acknowledged that my frog has great hair.

The funny thing about being *grateful* and *appreciative* is that the more grateful you are, the more you will FIND to be grateful for. The Universe always gives you more of that upon which you FOCUS. By appreciating Chris more, even for something as simple as having a nice head of hair, I began to focus more and more on his other good traits.

Before long, he began to show his appreciation for me even more and our marriage started to grow. It really wasn't about me finding a way to change him. I wasn't changing him. What was happening was that by being more positive with my thoughts and actions, he discovered the girl he had originally fallen in love with and that made him WANT to change. Now, after 28 years, we are still acting like newlyweds.

Here is another example: I began to focus on my appreciation for the pick-up truck I was driving. I had "inherited it" from my daughter when she went to college. Because I appreciated what I had, I got more! It wasn't long before I found myself driving a Mercedes convertible, which I really love and appreciate! Once again, connecting with Source and FEELING my appreciation worked out pretty well, don't you think?

Then there's our home. I focused on being grateful for being able to live in my mom's basement and, before long, we were able to move into a very nice rental home with a small pool. I focused on being grateful for that home and now we own our million-dollar dream home.

And, it's not just me. Using these simple and very enjoyable techniques **on a daily basis,** has enabled Chris' business to prosper as never before. Many of my friends and lifestyle coaching clients have experienced the same successes in **all** areas of their lives.

How is This Possible?

The reasons are clear. We're following the Universal Laws of Success. These laws, especially the Law of Attraction, are as real and unbending as the law of gravity. Dr. Michael Beckwith, who was featured in the movie *The Secret* says, "It doesn't matter whether you are a good person or a bad person, if you jump off a building you WILL fall."

The Law of Attraction is real. Laws don't work *some of the time.* They are iron clad and work ALL of the time, every time. All you have to do is access your Universal Power **daily** and get the Law on your side! If you're not where you'd like to be... or where you THINK you should be, then start working WITH the law. Now is the time to change.

Start by protecting your mind vigilantly. Only allow positive and uplifting information into your thoughts. Understand that whatever we focus on grows. If we watch violent movies, violence will become our way of coping. If we watch comedies, we will learn to resolve conflicts with humor. Resolve to watch more spiritual, inspiring films or comedies. Chris laughs at how he enjoys "Chick Flicks" now, and says I've ruined him forever... and he LOVES it!

Stay away from the newspapers and stop watching the news. If you must, you can check the headlines or important issues online.

Evaluate your relationships. Do your friends support you and look for the best in their own lives? Associating with friends who put you down or tell you that you dream too big will actually keep you right where you are. Choose your friends carefully and if you are the smartest, most successful person in your circle, find new, more positive and successful friends.

Make sure that everything you think and do leaves you feeling positive and grateful. Flood your mind with positive, feel-good books, movies, and friends. Listen to "The Genie Within" by my husband Chris Douglass (*www. GenieWithin.com*). Another resource that we base so much of our work on is Dan Millman's *The Way of the Peaceful Warrior.* Visit our Web site for more suggestions at *www.FitTips.com.* It's time you claimed the life of your dreams. I've done it, my clients have done it, and you can, too!

Andy Ebon, *"The Wedding Marketing Authority,"* is a public speaker, podcaster, marketing expert, and business coach. Andy's expertise reflects more than a decade in Internet marketing preceded by 25 years in the disc jockey entertainment industry.

In early 2007, Andy turned his focus to educating wedding professionals to successfully connect with brides and grooms through creative and effective marketing and communication. His highly successful Wedding Marketing Blog ranks in the *top one percent of all blogs* (source: Alexa).

For blog, business, and wedding marketing expertise contact Andy at: 888-275-0922, 702-227-9926, or visit his sites at:

www.TheWeddingMarketingBlog.com
www.WeddingMarketing.net

Chapter Four

Blogging Your Way To Business Success

Andy Ebon

Did you know there is ONE THING you can do to set your business apart, drive traffic and essentially secure your success – regardless of where you live and work, or what happens to the economy?

If you're not blogging yet, either because you don't know what it is, you are not comfortable with it, or you don't realize how powerful it is, don't despair. As quickly as you can read this chapter, you can discover how easy it is to blog.

Blogs: Text Book Definition
Blogs (short for web log) are a ubiquitous part of the "New Social Media." Simply put, a blog is an online journal, maintained by an individual, business owner, or company representative. Blogs are self-service websites that enable you to write articles, post pictures, and field

comments and responses in a variety of easy software scenarios.

Blogs: Definition for Deep Thinkers

If utilized to its fullest, a blog is more than a new medium or method of communication. ***It's the online face, personality, and soul of your company.*** It is the vehicle with which you can communicate with your various communities: Prospects, customers, employees, media, or, simply, the casual observer. Blogging is a form of direct public relations, driven by you, to facilitate numerous business goals.

It cannot be emphasized enough that blogs are no longer merely "recommended as a good thing to do." Virtually every communications expert will tell you blogs are now a *mandatory* part of your communications arsenal.

Reasons for Blogging

Whether your primary focus is Business-to-Business or Business-to-Consumer, you have the opportunity to become a thought and discussion leader without a major investment in software or hardware. Anyone with an Internet browser can create and maintain a blog.

Straightforward reasons for blogging include:

- Build up to product releases
- Service updates and advisories
- Tips in your area of expertise
- Tips about the optimum use of your products

- Building brand or product awareness
- Improving search engine traffic to your website

Keys to Business Blogging Success

Blogs are a search-engine-friendly complement to an existing website. Moreover, blogs address one major weakness of most websites. Most businesses don't update their websites often enough, which hurts them in search engine rankings. Blogs, on the other hand, can easily be updated daily or weekly.

Blogging Software

There are three major blogging software platforms and they all live on the Internet, not on your computer. They are: **Wordpress, Blogger, and TypePad. Wordpress** is free, open-source software. **Blogger,** which is owned by Google, is free; **TypePad** has a free version with basic features. More advanced versions of **TypePad** are available through paid subscription.

Blogger is the easiest to use, especially if you are just getting started. **TypePad** is nicely self-contained. However, the overall best choice is **Wordpress.** All three products are accessed from any computer's browser (Internet Explorer, Firefox, Safari, etc.) You can update your blog from your office or an Internet café in Paris... or virtually anywhere in the world where you can access the internet.

A major benefit of **Wordpress** is that it is set up in a file on your website. For example: *www.weddingmarketing.net/blog.* A blog, working within your website is helpful, because *all the activity that your blog attracts counts as traffic to your website.* That facilitates better search engine ranking on Google and other search engines.

For that reason alone, **WordPress** is recommended by serious practitioners. Many hosting companies provide easy, 1-click installation of **WordPress** within their hosting packages. Just ask!

Accidental Search Engine Optimization

When writing about different aspects of your business, you will use **keywords** in your posts that prospects use in searches. You will do it by accident. If you write about real estate, REO, bank loans, mortgages and the like, having those keywords in visible text and on the screen, automatically creates search-engine-friendly copy within an industry.

How Search Engine Friendly is Blogging?

A simple example is my business blog: "The Wedding Marketing Blog" (*www. TheWeddingMarketingBlog.com*), which I launched in February 2007. Its "true" address is within my website (*www.WeddingMarketing. net/blog*). It was conceived to position me as the Wedding Marketing Expert, sharing chunks of information, advice, conjecture and suggestions about wedding marketing. This blog is strictly a business-to-business niche site.

It further publicizes my public speaking and also lays the groundwork for a weekly podcasting program, "Wedding Marketing Radio." My blog, more than anything else, is the most effective marketing tool for elevating my visibility as the leading Wedding Industry Business and Marketing Coach.

Today, both the blog activity and my website are ranked in the top one percent of all blogs and websites (Source: Alexa). More important than numbers, however, is its growing community, stretching around the globe. Enter the phrase "wedding marketing" in Google and you'll find ME - again and again.

On any given day, a blog can garner dozens, hundreds, even thousands of readers. What one can't predict is when the next client will be reading your blog or what might pique their interest.

For Whom Should You Write?
What Should You Write About?

Blogs are read by: prospects, peers, customers, industry contacts, and the media. Write for them, since they are your audience. Ask yourself, "What would interest *them?*"

Resist the temptation to make blogging an infomercial – or completely self-serving. You will not gain a loyal audience that way. The content balance should be roughly 75% informational and 25% promotional. Angles that entertain and interest a reader may focus on another person in your industry or business, not necessarily your business (unless it's a specific product, product line or star employee).

Write about the great collaboration you worked on last week. Focus on an employee... a team member who solved a major problem, saved your company money in development, and ultimately saved your customer (the reader) money.

Permission Marketing vs. Interruption Marketing

World Class marketer, Seth Godin, coined the phrase "Permission Marketing" in one of his early books. It is the opposite of "Interruption Marketing," which occurs in TV and radio, for example, when commercials interrupt programming. When you are flipping the pages of a magazine or newspaper, you are interrupted by ads.

However, blogging is an example of communication with permission. People who discover your blog and find your subject matter interesting or helpful can elect to return, periodically or they can elect to subscribe, either by email notification or RSS, which stands for "Really Simple Syndication." Readers who choose email notification will receive a single email, usually daily or weekly, with the subject lines of your latest posts. One click on an interesting topic, and they are back at your blog – reading your latest message.

RSS is the "quiet giant of permission." RSS readers are contained within various email software, browsers, and stand alone RSS Readers. When someone subscribes to blogs via RSS, they receive notification about new posts in real time. If, at some future date, a subscriber loses interest in a particular blog, one click will unsubscribe them from RSS or email notification.

Nuts and Bolts of Blogging

From a technical standpoint, learning to blog is easy. If you can write a document in Microsoft Word and know how to upload a photo, you have the minimum technical skills to author a blog. The bigger challenge is writing on a consistent basis. Just once or twice weekly is fine. You can even write several posts in one day and schedule them to post live on different days in the future. This feature allows you to keep your blog working while you're on the beach, away from your desk, or simply busy.

Before starting your blog, read lots of other blogs. Read industry-specific blogs, your competitors' blogs, or blogs about your favorite hobby or sports team. You will quickly develop a reader-perspective and understand the importance of writing for the audience in an entertaining and informative way.

Delegating Elements of Your Blog

You are able to assign different levels of access to the blog: Publisher, Editor, Writer, etc. Using this hierarchy, you can distribute the blogging load among several contributors within your organization. An editor or publisher has the last word on proofreading any article before it's published.

Comments on Your Blog

Whether complimentary, constructive criticism, or combative, comments show readers are interested. You have flexibility as to how comments are posted. Many bloggers choose to use the **moderation setting** to **approve posts** before they become visible to all readers. There are also anti-spam tools to practically eliminate inappropriate spam comments.

Designing Your Blog

Unless you have the design skills and interest, you need not become a designer. There are many free templates for **WordPress** blogs. Some outstanding templates are available from many sources for under $100. If you prefer a custom design, there are specialists who can provide that service, too.

Plugins for Your Blog

There are many gadget programs, called plugins, available for **WordPress**; most of them are free. Plugins perform specific tasks that provide extra features for the reader or the blogger. A database of plugins can be found on *WordPress.org.*

Your Action Plan:
- Read a variety of blogs
- Examine blog software choices (WordPress recommended)
- Set up a test blog and tinker with it
- Write your blog for a couple of months

When your blog has some content and a good rhythm of posting, publicize it. For additional resources and information, visit me at: *www.WeddingMarketing.net/popblogging.*

Amanda Gore is a highly regarded business speaker on how emotional intelligence is a key in successfully bringing about change in today's business settings. Her expertise is in transforming the spirit of people and cultures by changing attitudes, improving relationships, connecting people, managing change, leadership, innovation, and team dynamics.

A native Aussie, Amanda has a unique ability to connect, entertain, educate, and involve the audience so that they laugh while learning effective, new skills that have a long-term impact.

Author of four books and several video and audio training programs, Amanda has a bachelor's degree in physical therapy, a major in psychology, and expertise in ergonomics, stress management, group dynamics, neuro-linguistics, and occupational health. E-mail Amanda at *Amanda@AmandaGore.com* or visit *www.amandagore.com.*

Chapter Five

The Joy of Change

Amanda Gore

"Problems cannot be solved at the same level of thinking that created them" --Albert Einstein

It seems an oxymoron to put joy and change in the same sentence. But my next mission is to help people understand that change is possible and can be joyful. We know change is the only constant in today's world of complexity and chaos, and that the bulk of a leader's job is to facilitate changes in people's behaviors.

The good news is that research in a field called neuroplasticity has become popular and proves that we CAN change! We are NOT hard wired, as previously believed.

The Brain and the Power of Focus and Attention
Essentially, neuroplasticity describes the brain's ability to set up new connections. Everything in life is about connections....at a brain and heart level. At 23, I was a new,

enthusiastic, and excited physical therapist, working in a neurological ward. I have no idea how I knew about neuroplasticity, but I did!

I used to explain to my stroke patients that the first time they managed to control or regain an isolated movement a tiny scratch would be etched on their brain. Each time they repeated this movement or action the scratch would become deeper and deeper until it was so deep that the movement became automatic. At that point, they would not have to think or work so hard to make that movement.

This is in essence what neuroplasticity does. If we focus our attention on what it is we want to change and repeat it frequently, we can make new connections and lay down new pathways. The more we do it, the easier it becomes, until finally we don't even have to think about doing it – it becomes automatic.

An accountant has a bigger, more connected brain in the area of formulae and numbers than I do. A surgeon has a highly developed dexterity part of the brain. A great salesperson has a huge "relationship corner"! A jeweler has exceptional eyesight and precision hand movements. In other words, if you spend a long time learning about and practicing a skill, your brain will have different 'lumps and bumps' than someone who specializes in another area!

Likewise, if we continually focus on the negative aspects of anything, THOSE connections and neural pathways are reinforced – until THEY become our automatic response. Before you know it, everything in your life becomes negative and you are officially a pessimist! This is why it is of the utmost importance that we pay attention to what we focus on in life – good or bad.

Learning

If we want someone to do something different, we have to give them enough information, knowledge, and training to feel supported and confident. Learning new things that are completely different and complex - things that we have never done before - is the way to keep our brains young and vital.

I had always had a dream to play the harp. I loved harp music but knew nothing about it. When my Mum died, she left me some money and so I bought a harp. I was blessed to find an extraordinary teacher, Linda, who was a saint. Imagine teaching a 53-year old woman who had never played a musical instrument before! I didn't even know what a flat or a melody was! All this totally new learning gobbled up oxygen and glucose as my prefrontal cortex – the part we use to learn new things – worked overtime. That is why many of us find change so uncomfortable – because of the energy expenditure to keep the prefrontal cortex fed while it processes, learns, and makes new connections. It's a physical reaction but it can seem more like an emotional one.

I'm still learning and it is amazing to me how tired I am at the end of just sitting in one spot trying to coordinate 3,000 things that my teacher does effortlessly and brilliantly! She sounds fabulous; I sound "different"!

Letting Go Of Judgment

Judging ourselves often blocks our learning and capacity to change! Our perceptions and beliefs about ourselves shape our reality. What we expect to happen and what really happens are often very different things. I believe it helps us to replace judgment with reverence.

See yourself and others with reverence. Reverence means we see the spark of divinity in every person we meet – no matter who they are. We hold them in awe and wonder and acknowledge that they are amazing beings. Sometimes we have to keep reminding ourselves, but if you can truly view someone else with reverence, you will be stunned at the difference it will make in all your dealings with them.

Never Give Up

It's easy and natural for most of us to give up when the going is tough. The work we actually have to do to effect that change is energy expensive. It takes effort, commitment, perseverance, patience, and discipline. And so we perceive it as hard – especially if we don't see the value in it for ourselves.

We give up – often just before a change is cemented or we are able to reap the benefits of our efforts. Imagine how wonderful it would be if we could face change with cheerful enthusiasm! Having faith that things will work out, doing our best, being optimistic, and staying cheerfully engaged throughout the whole process makes change a joyful process!

Change is a choice; choosing to be engaged and connected; choosing to participate; choosing to serve rather than just seeking personal gain. As leaders, we need to choose to present change in a way that touches people's hearts AND minds. We must give them the skills, knowledge, confidence and courage to be successful with new changes. Our brains need to see/feel/hear the changes quickly, so our hearts are encouraged and we stay motivated to participate and be engaged. Change your perceptions first and your world and others around you will change.

More than a life coach, **Jim Fannin** is a "change your life" coach. His thought management system *empowers* people to *swiftly* be the best they can be without inconvenience. Period!

Jim has 35+ years of experience as an author, educator, raconteur, life strategist and sports and business consultant. He has trained individuals and companies from 36 industries and coached more than 150 professional athletes from eight sports in peak performance.

Today, Jim divides his time between public speaking, personal coaching, corporate consulting, writing, and his Think Like a Champion Foundation. He is based in Chicago, IL. For more information, visit *www.JimFannin. com* or call 877-210-2001.

Chapter Six

Think Like A Champion

Jim Fannin

My name is Jim Fannin. I coach champions.

You are "locked" in the moment as you walk down the 18th fairway toward the green. Your approach is now lying four feet from the pin. You are purposeful yet calm. There is a feeling that nothing can go wrong. Time stands still. Your eyes are dilated and your skin sensitivity is heightened. A chemical cocktail floods your blood stream giving you inordinate accuracy, power, and consistency. Intuition rules. You are in the NOW. You are in the "Zone," the peak performer's mindset.

This champion's mindset is <u>NOT</u> limited to sports. You can be in the "Zone" during a business deal, sales call, or even reading a book.

Five intangibles, when balanced at a high level, attract the Zone... the mindset of a champion. They are:

Self-discipline: This is the willingness and commitment to stay with a task(s) that leads to a goal(s) and ultimately your vision. Every champion I've coached had a clear vision of his or her future. A self-disciplined performer has a plan to achieve the dream with synchronized strategy and tactics. This person is persistent and purposeful in all of their actions.

> *Tip: Think Abnormally. Most of us were trained to go from A to B to achieve our goals. However, if you have an abnormal dream you must think in an abnormal way. First, see B in your mind's eye. See it as if it is so. Then illuminate a pathway chronologically in reverse from B back to A. Now, like an airport runway at night, the pathway is lit so that you can walk straight to your goal. If you get off track, you have an illuminated pathway as a marker.*

Concentration: This is the ability to focus mental and physical energy on the task(s) that lead to a goal(s) and ultimately your vision. With blinders, the champion stays the course with simplicity and persistence. Like a cheetah that may track its prey for hours, a peak performer's concentration is unwavering until the task is completed. I eat now... thinks the cheetah. Keep it simple. Be the cheetah!

> ***Tip: The 90-second Rule.*** *The next time you go home or to the office after an absence of two or more hours, prepare to give your family or co-workers your undivided attention for the first 90 seconds. This time has more impact than spending hours with them later. You may have to make that last phone call in the driveway or clear your brain before you walk through the door. Give all your undivided attention and energy to the greeting. The 90-Second Rule lets you concentrate on what matters... people.*

Optimism: This is the belief and expectancy that the task(s) will lead to a goal(s) and ultimately your vision. Optimism becomes your constant while all around there are variables of chaos. Changing conditions and circumstances, unreliable people as well as faulty planning can deter most people. But not the Optimist! This person is a world class problem solver. Every question has an answer. And every answer takes you closer to your vision.

> ***Tip: Framing.*** *Bolster your optimism by seeing what you want and NOT what you don't want. Shut your eyes, relax your jaw, and see it in your mind. See it as you fall asleep and when you awaken. In this semi-drowsy, alpha brainwave*

mindset, your subconscious mind is most fertile for suggestion. Within ten days of framing your day with one purpose, your subconscious mind will begin to control all that you want. Coincidence and synchronicity will occur.

Relaxation: This is being comfortable mentally and physically with the task(s) that leads to a goal(s) and ultimately your vision. A relaxed performer is free from worry, anxiety, and frustration. They look like they're not even trying.

> ***Tip: Breathe Like a Baby.*** *Do you ever get the butterflies before an important meeting or public speaking performance? The butterflies are when blood vessels in your stomach constrict, diverting blood to the brain for clarity, and to the large muscles for inordinate strength, speed, and agility. Your body is preparing to attract the Zone. The following relaxation tool is how a baby breathes to go to sleep and how you can relax in less than a minute:*

- Unhinge your jaw and relax your face and neck.
- Place either hand over your stomach near your belly button.
- With each inhale draw your belly button closer to backbone.

- With each exhale move your belly button away from backbone.
- After 6-8 breathes you'll feel your shoulders relax and tension fade.

Enjoyment: This is about loving what you do and doing what you love. Champions have satisfaction and pleasure while performing the task(s) that lead to the goal(s) and finally the vision. They love the ride!

> *Tip: **Be a Kid Again.** Why did you learn more from birth to five years old than the rest of your life combined? What prompted this super learning? My research from 1974-1979 with thousands of children ages three to six years old revealed your enjoyment level was awesome because of the following:*
>
> - *The past wasn't thought about unless an adult forced you. "I told you not to do that." Your future thoughts were short term. "We'll get ice cream later."*
> - *You exercised **Free Will** daily.*
> - *Conversation wasn't full of innuendos, rumor, gossip, and/or assumptions. Everything was asked up-front without concern of embarrassment or shame. "Why is your skin darker than mine?"*
> - *You didn't worry; you lived the majority of your day in the NOW. And*

*when you played, you never thought
technique. You just played.*

- *You thought you could do anything.
  Everything was possible. Water...
  heights... speed... No problem!*
- *You loved rolling down a hill...
  making a snow angel... going up the
  slide... singing loud... laughing...
  milk moustaches... make-believe...
  birthdays... parades... puppies...
  seeing your cousins... learning to
  whistle...*
- *You genuinely loved yourself, family,
  and life.*

*Basically, you lived in or near the Zone. I
promised myself that when I departed this earth
a kid would die in my old body. Rekindle super-
learning. Increase the enjoyment level in your
daily performances and remember this:* **Be a
kid again!**

These five keys of **S**elf-discipline, **C**oncentration,
Optimism, **R**elaxation, and **E**njoyment form
the acronym of S.C.O.R.E. So... how's *your*
S.C.O.R.E.? Which intangible is your weakest
link? You may need self-discipline in golf and
relaxation in business. Next week, after the
conditions and circumstances change, your
weak links could be reversed. Remember:
You are only as strong as your weak link in
S.C.O.R.E. Manage these five intangibles at a
balanced, high state and the phenomenon of
the Zone will appear.

With awareness and practice maybe you'll be like Michael Jordan of the former world-champion Chicago Bulls. He said to me, "Jim, I know the Zone. I can put it on like an overcoat."

It's time to get in the Zone! Think like a champion.

Tana Goertz is an internationally recognized speaker, author, entrepreneur, leader, and success coach. She is best known as a finalist in the reality television shows *The Apprentice – Season Three* and *Fear Factor*, and she is the international spokesperson for the Bedazzler.

Donald Trump stated that Tana has, "that rare combination of laid-back charm and razor sharp execution. She doesn't put up with nonsense."

Tana combines a "can-do" attitude, spirit, and energy with vision and execution to propel individuals beyond their current limitations. Her motivational topics include leadership, entrepreneurial mentorship, personal development, seizing opportunity, and becoming successful in every aspect of life.

Tana can be reached at 515-707-7580 or by email at *tana@heytana.com* or visit her website at *www.heytana.com*.

Chapter Seven

I Was Born To Sell;
What Were You Born To Do?

Tana Goertz

Have you ever stopped to think about what you were born to do? From a very young age, it was obvious that I was born to sell. The minute that I learned how to talk, I was selling my family on everything – from convincing my sisters to let me take my shower first to talking my mother into making lasagna. My "professional" sales career started at age nine, when I convinced my parents to let me sell a telephone gadget door-to-door. For most kids, this would have lasted only a day; for me, it was my first taste of real money, so I stuck with it. I made a profit of more than $4,000 after repaying my parents' initial investment.

This drive continued throughout high school and into college when the impossible happened – I was outsold! My first husband convinced me that he couldn't live without me, and that we would have a wonderful life if I married him. While painting this wonderful picture, he also sold me on NOT achieving my original dreams – finishing college and having a career. When relating this period of my life to others, I'm always stunned to hear how many people have similar stories of putting their dreams and aspirations on hold to fulfill someone else's.

After eight years of marriage, I took a serious assessment of my life and realized that I wasn't being the person that I was born to be. I knew that I would never be able to accomplish what I needed to in that situation. I left my husband and transitioned from a life of wealth and glamour to living in my parents' basement with my two small children. Luckily, my family understood my rationale and was extremely supportive – they realized how important it was to not have my children grow up seeing me unsatisfied and unfulfilled in my life.

Taking a Leap of Faith
Rather than giving in to fear and anxiety about the future, I decided to take a leap of faith and trust my core competency – selling. I began by working in my family's designer clothing consignment store, and added to business significantly by identifying a need for furniture consignment - pouncing on the opportunity. I also discovered Mary Kay. The lure of additional income and the constant competition within the sales force made for an ideal working environment. From the start,

I was consistently the top saleswoman in my region.

Years later, I met my current husband through one of my customers. Not only is Kurtis the man I have always dreamed of, but he is also very supportive of my goals and aspirations. After we married and settled into life in Iowa, I had another unique opportunity present itself to me – the chance to compete on *The Apprentice: Street Smarts vs. Book Smarts.*

A Star is Born

I knew that I would be up against more than 1,000,000 people to get a spot on the show, and that to be a stand-out I had to make an incredible audition video. To show my strengths and unique abilities I decided to sell Mary Kay cosmetics to men – more specifically, car dealers in Los Angeles. They not only lined up to buy my products, but I also received several job offers because of my incomparable selling abilities. The audition video captured a perfect picture – a unique, fearless, enthusiastic person, succeeding at what she was born to do.

While on *The Apprentice,* I was able to sell myself to Donald Trump and producer Mark Burnett. Week after week I was successful, and through the process, I learned a lot about myself. I was considered one of the best salespeople out of the "best of the best" in the business world. Again and again, Mr. Trump praised my presentation abilities. Many people couldn't believe that a mom from Iowa without a college degree could aggressively compete and win against those who had business degrees from some of the best schools in the country. In my journey, I discovered that my unique, fearless, optimistic attitude was a real asset and that I loved being the person that I was born to be.

In the end, I was the last contestant standing for the "Street Smarts" team, and the first and only person in the history of *The Apprentice* to make it to the finale without a college degree. When the show ended, I was faced with a challenge. For past contestants, appearing on the program had been the culmination of their careers. However, I saw it only as a stepping stone to the life that I wanted. I knew that I had an audience of more than 41 million viewers and would be going on a publicity tour as soon as the show aired, so in the interim I wrote and self-published a children's book titled *I'm Bigger Than This!* I had it on hand to plug while on the *Today Show, Conan O'Brien,* and many other national television shows.

In addition to the book, I was presented with two other major sales opportunities once the show had aired. The first was from the owner of the Bedazzler (a product I plugged in an episode), asking me to be their international spokesperson. I pounced on this opportunity and still represent this product today. The second opportunity was more subtle. As I said earlier, Mr. Trump repeatedly praised my presentation abilities. After an assessment of my strengths, I decided that a speaking career would best position me for future success.

Many of the producers and Mr. Trump said that I was unforgettable. I learned that many people like the product of "Tana" and I decided to BE the product that I sell now! Every day, I have the opportunity to sell my motivation, my inspiration, and my encouragement to those who are looking to take their lives to the next level and be the person THEY were born to be.

Doing What You Love

Confucius said, "Find a job you love and you'll never work a day in your life." I can honestly say that no matter how busy I am, I am doing what I love and what I was born to do, and it never feels like I'm working.

I hope that you have been thinking about my original question: What were you born to do? For some, it is apparent from day one. For others, it can be more subtle and develop over time. When I ask this question during speaking engagements, two things happen – the first is that something comes to mind almost immediately, i.e. "When I was young I wanted to be a ..." or "I've always been good at ..." The second, which usually comes in the same breath, is the excuse. "BUT I decided to have a family..." or "BUT I had to face reality..."

Over time, I have come to realize that the main reason most people haven't become the person they were born to be is the fear of failure.

So many people have denied their dreams, aspirations, and true selves because they are afraid that they will not be successful if they try. The fact is that if you never try, then you have a 100 percent guarantee that you are going to fail. Some people do try initially, and then stop at the first small failure they encounter, saying, "See! I told you this wouldn't work!" You will have failures and setbacks; trust me, I know. The important thing is to pick yourself back up, smile, and refocus on the end goal – there is always more than one path to success.

Many others feel that if they really expose their true selves, they might be rejected, shunned, or laughed at by the people that they love. It's always important to remember that if your loved ones are truly on your team, then they will support you no matter what or who you decide to be. Most of the time, we build up this rejection in our minds to be so much bigger than it truly is. Give your loved ones a chance to support you and I can guarantee they will surprise you.

Finally, I meet a lot of people who feel that their life has veered so off-course that they could never get back to accomplishing their dreams and goals. The best advice that I can give is from my personal situation with my first husband – take time to refocus and realize who you are and what you were born to do, and then make an action plan for how you're going to get there. There will be trade-offs and sacrifices along the way – but if you set your priorities and rely on your strengths, you will emerge victorious in the end.

People who are living their lives being the person they were born to be are happier, healthier, and are leading more fulfilling lives. Remember, this isn't an exclusive club; anyone can join! What opportunities keep arising in your life? What is it out there that keeps calling your name? It's time that you join in on the fun and start enjoying life today!

Les Brown is the leading authority on releasing human potential and enhancing lives. A renowned professional speaker, personal development coach, author and television personality, Les has risen to international prominence by capturing audiences with electrifying speeches... challenging audiences to live up to their greatness.

Les is the recipient of the National Speakers Association's highest honor and has been selected as one of the **World's Top Five Speakers** by Toastmasters International. Les trains others to become better communicators and speakers as well, currently working with more than 3,500 clients. His network enables all people to learn how to inspire others to new levels of achievement.

Les Brown is a master speaker who continues to reinvent himself to positively change the world. Visit *www.LesBrown.com* or call 800-733-4226.

Chapter Eight

"When Things Go Wrong, Don't Go With Them!"

Les Brown

Sometimes it seems as though life is getting tough. It is as if everything around us is collapsing... simply crumbling before our very eyes. Many people are uncertain about the future, money, relationships, health, and careers. In fact, some of us are beginning to question the very nature of life itself.

In uneasy times, as a world-renown motivator, my advice is simply this: *When things go wrong, don't go with them.* Have you watched the news lately? It's quite depressing isn't it? With all of this mess going on around us, you have to *monitor your mind and mouth.* I'm not oblivious to shocking headlines and a poor economy, but I can't consume myself with it because whatever you focus on the longest becomes the strongest.

Everyone has one friend who calls with nothing but bad news. I have to talk to people who see opportunities in the eye of the storm. Not the person who advises me to put my money under a mattress, or recommends taking self-defense classes because crime rates are increasing. I have to observe my surroundings for mental protection or else I'd be afraid to live!

What Happens Inside You

Elise Robinson said, "Things may happen around you and things may happen to you, but the only thing that matters is what happens in you." In the midst of chaos, you have to brace yourself, build your faith, feed your mind with positive materials, and seek opportunities you've never considered before. Who cares what the rest of the world is doing? You should be getting stronger, smarter, and strategizing to launch a new life, astonishing everyone with your success and tenacity.

In times like these, we have to look for opportunities and act fast like never before. Most of us have heard the expression, "Opportunity knocks." Well, I'd like to challenge that theory, because if opportunity REALLY knocked, most of us would answer the door! I agree with speaker Steve Duncan, who said, "Opportunity stands by silently, waiting for us to recognize it." And remember, opportunities may not come in cute, carefully wrapped packages. Opportunities may come in the way of defeats, setbacks, and failures.

Blessings in Disguise

Personally, I experienced some of the greatest opportunities when I was in despair. When I was fired from my job as a disc jockey, I felt betrayed and angry. I was ready to fight to get my job back, regardless of the fact that while I was at that job, I complained about being overworked and underpaid! Getting fired turned out to be a blessing in disguise. If I had not been fired, I might still be there today, and might never have discovered my true voice, talents and worldwide impact.

Dr. Robert Schuller said, "Tough times never last, but tough people do." Make no mistake about it, times may be tough, but you are tougher. What are the odds of surviving 400 million sperm? Those are the odds you beat to get here in the first place! You are resilient beyond your wildest imagination. Stop looking at the circumstances around you. As Tony Robbins would say, "Bring out the *Giant Within.*"

I hear you; *it's easier said than done,* right? Well, maybe. See, I found life so uncomfortable when I was leading an average life. I was broke, miserable, and angry at the world. But, it's never easy to do something different, something outside of your comfort zone.

In fact, people run and hide from challenges. I was one of them. To make my point easier, remember the story of *Jonah and the Whale?*

Jonah hid in the belly of a whale to avoid living up to higher expectations! How *easy* was that? One African Proverb says, "If there's no enemy within, the enemy outside can do us no harm." I believe we should get out of *our own* way; simply put, *Get Out of Your Head and Into Your Greatness.*

Finding Your True Self

Lastly, find your true self. We live within the conversations in our heads and the recommendations of others. For years, I operated as *DT*, which was my childhood nickname meaning, "the dumb twin." Believe it or not, I answered to it! I lived like the dumb twin; never taking risks, always getting into trouble, and never dreaming big. There was one person, a former teacher, who interrupted the years of negativity and low expectations for me by saying, "Never let someone else's opinion of you become your reality."

Again, *Get out of your head and into your greatness.* The *dumb twin* set low expectations for my life. My friends and neighbors, with their negative comments and discouraging words, had a toxic impact on my mind. How many negative voices do you have floating in your head? Here you are - extremely talented, but your spouse told you to "be realistic" when you shared your goals.

I can't say it enough; get out of your head! Forget about those doubts, obstacles, and fears; create a strategy.

• Take an hour a day to program your mind for success. Remember, information costs, but it pays for itself.

• Write down goals that will take you outside of your comfort zone.

• Read something positive everyday, particularly in the morning. How you spend the first 20 minutes of your day will determine the flow for the rest of the day.

• Finally, upgrade your relationships. Dr. Dennis Kimbro said, "If you are the smartest in your group of friends, get new friends."

These are very simple tips on getting ahead. Make it happen and make a difference!

Angelique Daniels' signature book, "Epigphany: a Health and Fitness Spiritual Awakening" is an inspiration for anyone who has ever battled weight or fitness issues. It wasn't long before she discovered that the "P.I.G." strategy she used to overcome her fitness challenges proved to have universal applications which can lead to success in other areas of life.

As a working, married mother of two, Angelique draws upon more than twenty-five years in management to inspire audiences with a refreshing outlook on balancing work and family. She holds a Bachelor's degree in Business from Eastern Michigan University.

Her life is an impressive testimonial that makes her a compelling and gifted speaker. Angelique speaks on health and wellness, success, and how we can each tap in to our spiritual gifts. Visit her website at *www.FatonSuccess.com*, e-mail her at *FATONSUCCESS@aol.com*, or call 702-271-3151.

Chapter Nine

Fat On Success

Angelique Daniels

I lost sixty pounds and ten dress sizes on my own. Accomplishing this and sharing my story with others sparked a desire in me to become a professional speaker. Now, every time I step on the platform to share my story, I am *living my dream!* My journey has been amazing, full of life lessons, hard work and "A-ha" moments.

My dream is to do something I love, help other people, and make money doing it. I am married and have two wonderful children. That can be a very fulfilling life. But, I always felt like something was missing.

Losing the weight was a catalyst for a much bigger plan. The fact that my overweight friends didn't share my joy in this accomplishment was an "A-ha" moment that changed my life. I realized that I was supposed to use this new-found power of self-control and discipline for good, not to flaunt it. I knew God was involved because as much as I loved to eat and knowing what a PIG I was, it could only have been divine intervention that assisted me - not just to lose weight, but also to write a book so I could share my story. Losing weight transformed me spiritually and physically.

Through self-reflection, I discovered my desire to share everything good in my life with others... whether or not they want to hear it! I think that makes me some kind of evangelist - YIKES! I realized that my true purpose is to inspire others by sharing my weight loss story and, more importantly, to encourage people to set bigger goals for themselves and reach their dreams, as I did.

The EPIGPHANY

"**E-PIG-PHA-NY**" is the title of my book, which I published in 2005. I created the term, defined as the exact moment you decide to do something about your weight. This moment is different from all those other times. Your mind is clear and you are totally focused. This is the first step in any weight loss plan.

An "**EPIPHANY**" is defined as "a sudden intuitive leap of understanding, especially through an ordinary but striking occurrence." Having this moment is the first step in achieving your goals and reaching your dreams.

To create your own epiphany, take inventory of your life and your spiritual gifts. If you don't know what your gifts are, analyze the compliments you receive. Often when you receive a compliment, it affirms a spiritual gift you possess. Do you use your gifts to achieve your dreams? Through prayer and meditation I got my answer and you can, too. I began working on my dream of becoming a professional speaker so that I could share my strategy for success and motivate others.

The P.I.G. Strategy

I originally created the "P.I.G." strategy to lose weight, but soon discovered that it works just as effectively for achieving ANY goal. I chose this acronym because my eating habits were similar to that of a PIG! I ate with no regard for quality or quantity. The three steps of my P.I.G. strategy are:

1. Portion Control
2. Investigate
3. Get moving

1. Portion Control

I lost a significant amount of my weight by controlling my portions. Get a smaller plate! Think before you eat. Eat until you are SATISFIED - not FULL.

2. Investigate

Educate yourself on the facts of food and nutrition. There is no excuse for ignorance today, especially with the Internet. When I began my weight loss journey, I didn't know a carb from a calorie. Once you understand the effects that BAD foods have on your body, it will help you to eat less of the bad foods; you'll start to make better, smarter, and healthier choices.

3. Get Moving

Sorry folks. There is no magic pill. If you are serious about losing weight and becoming healthy, you have to exercise. You don't need to join a gym or buy equipment. I was not a fitness enthusiast at all, so I simply started by walking. I'd enjoy the breeze or the brilliance of nature. Find something that you enjoy that will not be a strain at first and, before you know it, you'll find yourself looking forward to doing it the next day. For a detailed account of my weight loss, pick up my book, *EPIGPHANY: A Health and Fitness Spiritual Awakening.*

I soon put my P.I.G. strategy to the test toward attaining my other goals. Remember, my dream is to do something I love, help people, and make money doing it. Here is how I used my P.I.G. strategy to achieve my next goal, and you can, too.

1. Portion Control

Here, portion control applies to TIME. How do you portion your day? Where can you find time to pursue your dream? As a wife, active mom, restaurant manager, dog owner, and home owner, how could I find the necessary time to pursue my dreams? I made a commitment to myself that I would watch very little television. That way, my family wouldn't feel cheated or threatened by my new activity. I work relentlessly on my dream for about three hours every night when my children go to bed. A little effort goes a long way.

Few people ever ask how long it took me to lose the weight. It took an entire year – at the rate of about a pound per week! Some weeks were better than others, but even a little consistent effort over a period of time adds up.

I started using more positive "self talk." Instead of creating chaos - endless errands, housework, and volunteering for everything, I now say that I create my own success. I am positioned to meet the right people, those who support and inspire me. By doing this, I am creating an environment where my dream can grow.

Feel like you're spinning your wheels? Start to make productive use of your time. Say "no" to activities that monopolize your time and energy with little ROI (return on your investment). If you want to manifest your dreams, your decisions must move you in that direction. Work on your dream everyday. You will be amazed at your progress at the end of each day, month, and year.

2. Investigate

Once you establish your goal, you need to investigate your area of interest. The Internet is an excellent source. My dream was to become a professional speaker. Through the Internet I discovered Toastmasters, a group designed to help you fine-tune your public speaking skills. I also researched various speakers, watching their videos online.

One night while working on my dream by doing research on the Internet, I found a speaker who lived near me who was doing exactly what I wanted to do. I emailed her, we met for coffee, and I hired her to be my mentor. Within just three months, I was living my dream more fully and sooner than I had imagined possible! With her help, coaching and encouragement, I was speaking to a group about my book and selling my products! Having a mentor will accelerate your success by opening doors and helping you to avoid costly, time-consuming mistakes. Investigate your field of interest, find a qualified mentor and you'll soon find yourself among the right people, in the right circumstances necessary for you to succeed.

3. Get Moving

I want to scream when I hear someone complain about their life yet do nothing to change it. You don't need money to research your dream, and many networking events are free. You do, however, need a burning desire to succeed, and the courage to step outside your comfort zone. Don't be afraid to try new things. Position yourself to receive your blessings. Every time I make an effort toward my dream, another door opens. Get up, get out, and GET MOVING!

Your Entourage

I love my family and friends dearly but sometimes they don't share my vision and I don't get the energy from them that I need to keep motivated. Be prepared to accept this. Seek out positive people who are on a similar path so you can learn, share and grow.

It's lonely when everyone is tired of hearing about your highs and lows. Early in my journey, I met Annie Lee, a very successful artist and now a dear friend of mine. She came from very humble beginnings and built her empire living her dream. I can never thank her enough for her encouragement. She taught me that there is no SECRET to success; you can have anything you want if you are willing to work hard, stay focused and believe in yourself.

Fuel your spirit by surrounding yourself with like-minded individuals. Keep the burning desire and your faith in God strong and you will get there. Live like a P.I.G. - FAT ON SUCCESS!

Dr. Tony Alessandra has a street-wise, college-smart perspective on business, having realized success as a former graduate professor of marketing, Internet entrepreneur, business author and keynote speaker. He earned his PhD in 1976, in Marketing, from Georgia State University.

Dr. Alessandra is the chairman of *BrainX. com*, a company that created the first Online Learning Mastery System™, the president of *AssessmentBusinessCenter.com*, a company that offers online 360° assessments, and a founding partner in TheCyranoGroup.com, a company that has successfully combined simple, cutting-edge technology and proven psychology to give salespeople the ability to build and maintain positive relationships with hundreds of clients and prospects.

Dr. Alessandra is a widely published author with 17 books translated into 50 foreign language editions. He has been recognized by Meetings & Conventions Magazine as "one of America's most electrifying speakers." 858-456-0028, *TA@Alessandra.com, www.Alessandra.com.*

Chapter Ten

Being the Best You Can Be

Dr. Tony Alessandra

I've heard it said that there are three kinds of people: those who make things happen, those who have things happen to them, and those who wonder "What happened?" I want to help you propel yourself into that first category.

You *can,* in large measure, take control of your destiny. You already have everything you need. Now, it's up to you to build the best you that is possible. Success does not come to those who wait—and it doesn't wait for anyone to come to it.

Below are seven self improvement ideas. You may find that some of them are more difficult to carry out as they require changing years of habit. I hope seeing these will grab your attention and launch you toward new levels of success.

Suggestion No. 1: You Are Who You Think You Are

Think of yourself as a successful person. Hold that positive image. What you see is what you become, so make "successful" a mandatory part of your private self-description. This is important because *you're* the first person you need to convince.

Having a winning self-image *precedes* success; it doesn't follow it. It's easy to fall prey to cynical or pessimistic thoughts and axioms, or to believe that some people were just born successful. But the truth is - that's nonsense. If those with so-called "natural ability" don't cultivate the right skills, they'll fall short of their potential.

Suggestion No. 2: Apathy vs. Enthusiasm

Enthusiasm - not apathy - makes the world go 'round. John Wesley, the famous founder of Methodism, was asked how he was able to attract such crowds when he preached. He replied, "I just set myself on fire and people will come from miles to watch me burn."

Being enthusiastic isn't merely talking energetically and gesturing wildly about your passion. It can take a quieter path. Maybe your enthusiasm is revealed by the earnestness and persistence with which you seek to get others involved, by your strength of commitment; or by your refusal to become discouraged.

Suggestion No. 3: Embrace Your Potential

Everyone has the potential to be influential. Look for available opportunities, regardless of magnitude. Art Fry was a 3M scientist singing in his church choir, having trouble marking his place in the hymnal.

He needed something that would be easy to see and would stay put, but be removable. He dreamed up an idea on his own time, and then convinced his firm's higher-ups of the commercial possibilities. The result: Fry could keep his place in the hymnal, and the world got Post-it Notes, now a ubiquitous office tool and practically a household word.

Suggestion No. 4: Never Rest on Your Laurels

Mark McCormack, an attorney who represented many successful pro athletes and whom *Sports Illustrated* once called "the most powerful man in sports," said that all his star performers shared an endless quest to improve. "They use any success, any victory, as a spur to greater ambition," McCormack wrote in *What They Don't Teach You at Harvard Business School*. "Any goal that is attained immediately becomes the next step toward a greater, more 'unreachable' one."

Perhaps you have already enjoyed some success. Terrific! But never rest on your laurels and become complacent. The winner's real edge lies in the mind - a mind that's committed to perpetual self-improvement.

Suggestion No. 5: Persistence Always Pays Off
The road to success may not be easy. Overcoming setbacks and occasional self-doubts will require patience and persistence. But it's important to keep moving toward your goal.

A friend of mine had a life-changing experience during a cross-country ski race in Minnesota. New to the area and trying to adapt to the local culture, he bought skis, practiced a bit, and entered an advanced competition. After the first quarter-mile in near-zero temperatures, he knew he was in over his head. He was soon alone in a frozen wilderness and his thoughts turned gloomily to fatigue and defeat.

His goal to finish in a few hours seemed hopeless as the cold seared his lungs and the exertion weakened his arms and legs. He thought of surrender, but his only way out was to keep skiing. He pushed aside the pain and pessimism and forged ahead.

He imagined a lodge with a roaring fire, a rescue vehicle racing to pick him up, and even fantasized that a helicopter might come to his rescue, but of course, no help came.

So he skied on until, at last, he came to a sign: FINISH LINE, 1/4 MILE. He couldn't believe it! Energized, he sprinted that last quarter mile and finished close to his original goal.

The moral, as my friend sees it, is to keep moving forward, refuse to give up, and stay as positive as you possibly can. That is how to achieve your goals.

Suggestion No. 6: Happiness is the Journey, Not the Destination

Much of our happiness or unhappiness is caused not by what happens, but by how we look at what happens; in other words, by our thinking habits. And habits can be changed.

It's possible to develop a mind-set that will allow you to interpret setbacks as positive opportunities. For starters, purge the words "I failed ..." from your vocabulary. Replace them with "I learned ..." to help your mind focus on the lessons involved.

Similarly, you might want to get in the habit of using "challenge" when others would say "problem," "I'll be glad to" instead of "I'll have to," and "I'm getting better at ..." rather than "I'm no good at ..."

The subliminal effect of changing even a few words can prompt your mind to come up with creative solutions rather than dreading or fleeing the problem.

Suggestion No. 7: Write Your Obituary

Writing your obituary is a marvelous exercise in goal-setting. Take your time and include many details.

Your obituary can become your script, telling who you were, what you did, and how well you were liked. Reflecting on how you'd like to be remembered can help you to decide how you want to live – what kind of person you want to be, what you want to accomplish, what a good friend or partner you were and how you behaved in crisis. Write it. But understand that the only real way to have the sort of obituary you want is to start *living* the way you'd like to be remembered.

In Conclusion ~ The Best Things in Life Aren't Things

It's been said that success is getting what you want, but happiness is wanting what you get. Perspective can be easy to lose.

Seek to increase your success. Try to become the most effective person you can be. Work at making a good first impression and projecting a positive image—but also try to retain self-awareness.

Look around you; *think* about how you appear to others; *be alert* to the impression you're creating or trying to create. If you try too hard to impress, or come on too strong or too insensitively, you'll often end up creating a negative impression.

The surest way to success can sometimes be as simple as putting others first. Reportedly, one New York cab driver makes $30,000 more a year in tips than other cabbies. He offers passengers their choice of newspapers, beverages, and snacks. He asks what kind of music they'd prefer, and does his best to make his customers comfortable. In hectic, brusque Manhattan, his small acts of decency make him stand out.

People with the most effective images often are those who are the least obtrusive about it. In fact, sometimes it's a simple act or gesture of courtesy—like offering your full name when you see someone who may possibly have forgotten it. Maybe it's a short, sincere "thank you" note, or saying something nice about someone in front of their boss.

If never made, these gestures probably wouldn't be missed; that's why they're so obvious when you make them. But, being a genuinely good person who cares about others and who does things because they are the right things to do, may be the ultimate key to increasing your success.

Always do right because, as Mark Twain said, that will gratify some people and astonish the rest.

This chapter has been adapted from Dr. Tony Alessandra's book, *Charisma (Business Plus, Hachette Book Group, 1998)*.

Stormie Andrews has served as director of sales and marketing for a multimillion dollar organization. He has been recognized consistently for his award-winning career in sales and sales management and for his role as a sales trainer and company spokesperson.

He holds Certification from the esteemed Society of NLP as a Licensed Practitioner of Neuro-Linguistic Programming. Stormie is also a Certified Business Coach, an active member of Toastmasters International, and a Master Graduate of Rapport Leadership International. Stormie is an expert source for many news agencies across the country, including NBC, NPR and FOX.

Visit *www.StormieAndrews.com* to learn how you can improve your company's communication skills and increase sales through Stormie's NLP-inspired Sales and Communication Consulting with advanced NLP training.

E-mail Stormie at *Stormie@StormieAndrews.com* or call 888-910-7770.

Chapter Eleven

Stormie's Communication Nation
The Psychology behind Effective
Communication

Stormie Andrews

Each of us has been misunderstood at one time or another. For many of us, these moments of discord can have a significant impact on our life or business. Have you ever felt as though you and another person were on different pages, a situation where you were hearing one thing and the other person had a totally different perspective? It doesn't have to be that way. By applying "Stormie's Communication Nation," you can improve your life, generate more sales, and build rapport more quickly, all by improving your level of communication with business associates and loved ones.

To become the powerful communicator that you know you can be, you need an insight into how your brain processes information. I will show you how to make it easier for others to understand you and grasp your concepts. I will tell you how recognizing patterns in a person's behavior will reveal his or her preferred way of communication. Once you are able to identify how others think and process information, you will have the ability to understand them with clarity. You will gain a better understanding of *Visual, Auditory,* and *Kinesthetic* thinking patterns. You will become more aware of an individual's voice tone, word selection, and body language and you will gain a vivid understanding of his or her mental picture. So, fasten your seatbelt and let's get started.

The first thing that must be told is how the brain processes information. To illustrate my command of the thought process, I will tell you what you are thinking right now. You have the urge to skip this part and jump ahead. Well, don't! This information is integral to your study of effective communication, and will pay big dividends once you understand it. You have to build a strong foundation before you can construct your penthouse.

To be a successful communicator, you must understand the difference between the conscious and non-conscious minds. This will help you accept and utilize the communication behaviors that others are displaying. So, what's the difference between your conscious and non-conscious mind? Studies suggest that your conscious mind has the ability to process only about seven bits of information at any given moment and that you get to decide what to process and what not to process. Quite simply, anything that you are currently aware of at this very moment is part of your conscious mind and thoughts. Your non-conscious mind is everything else—what you're not aware of right now. Your non-conscious mind allows you to go about normal activities such as how to walk and chew gum at the same time... or how to drive home without actually thinking about where to turn.

The nice thing about your brain is that it's very easy to train (unlike a puppy!) Teaching your brain to recognize – and send - effective communication signals is a lot like upgrading the software on your computer. Once you know the precise information that you want your brain to process, you simply transfer this data into your conscious behaviors and thoughts. If you repeat this process enough times, these actions will become second nature to you and will also become a fundamental part of your non-conscious behavior. An example of how quickly something can become part of non-conscious behavior is the first time your hand came into contact with a flame. Your brain received a message that said, "HOT—this hurts. Don't do it again, dummy!" In fact, it is quite possible that your brain recorded lots of other information in that one instance, such as data reflecting the amount of heat in relation to the proximity of the flame or the smell associated with something burning. Whatever the case, your brain became conscious of fire, and your brain's internal software received an upgrade.

As a consequence, you NEVER have to think about the effects of touching fire again!

To communicate effectively, we have to understand how to upgrade our brain's hard drive. As mentioned earlier, the conscious portion of our mind will process only about seven bits of information at any given time. We use all forms of communication when it comes to selling, being effective on the job, being tactful in marriage, nurturing our children, etc. So ask yourself, what seven bits are you usually conscious of? What seven bits SHOULD you be conscious of?

All too often we tend to focus only on the verbal part of communication, or our words, and therefore overlook very important details. Research has shown that words typically account for just seven percent of their message when people communicate with one another. Vocal influences, or the tone of one's voice, make up about 38 percent, and body language, such as our posture, gestures, and eye contact, account for about 55 percent. When you're listening to someone and can focus on their entire message – including their words, tone of voice, and body language, you will discover greater clarity in their message and meaning. In other words, you will improve your ability to understand what they are trying to say.

People tend to use preferred representational systems when they speak, usually falling into one of these three categories: Visual (seeing),

Auditory (hearing), or Kinesthetic (feeling). You can determine other peoples' preferred systems by becoming aware of the verbs, adjectives, and adverbs they use when speaking. When you match their preferred system, you can establish rapport more quickly. Understanding another person's system allows you to communicate with them more effectively. Matching a person's system during conversation will reduce miscommunication by allowing the other person to hear your message without having to translate your message internally. It's like being from two different countries – yet being able to understand each other, even without the help of an interpreter.

HINT: If you're often misunderstood, read this chapter over and over again! The more energy the other person spends on translating your message, the less computing power they have to grasp what you are saying. When communicating, make it easy for others to understand you. Use the same representational systems on others as they use on you. You will also establish rapport by matching and modeling behaviors of the person you're communicating with. Mirror their body language, voice tone, and speech rate. Listen for their representational system and utilize it. Paraphrase what they say, because it's always a good idea to summarize a speaker's message for better understanding. Good listening skills require you to reflect back the speaker's message in his or her own representational system.

The following are some examples of Visual, Auditory, and Kinesthetic words and phrases.

- Visual words: Watch, see, illustrate, view, look, dim, glare, stare, brilliant, bright, envision, perceive.
- Visual phrases: I SEE what you are saying; I'll WATCH for change; Let me ILLUSTRATE this; I understand your point of VIEW.
- Auditory words: Hear, listen, groan, cry, voice, vibration, accent, ring, loud, resounding, express, recall.
- Auditory phrases: I HEAR what you're saying; We need to TALK about this; Please VOICE your concerns; Everything just CLICKED.
- Kinesthetic words: Touch, feel, grab, rub, tackle, hard, soft, warm, cold, relaxed, shiver, impress, clumsy.
- Kinesthetic phrases: I want you to FEEL the quality; this is built as SOLID as a ROCK; Do you have a GRASP of it?

Remember that the conscious mind can concentrate on only a limited amount of information at any given time. Improve your effectiveness by making your message easy for others to comprehend and understand. Use the other person's representational system to your advantage, and communicate in ways that make it easy for them to understand you.

- *Listen* for the entire message. *Look* for both verbal and non-verbal meanings. *Listen* for the speaker's *concepts*, *vision*, and *feelings*.

- Build rapport quickly by matching others' representational systems, body language, voice tone, and pace.
- Train your conscious mind to observe the representational system that others are using when they speak. Use THEIR representational system as part of your speech while talking with them. With enough repetition and practice this technique will become an automatic part of your non-conscious behavior.
- When speaking to groups, make sure you incorporate a nice mix of Visual, Auditory, and Kinesthetic words. This type of mix will keep your audience in tune with your message, allowing your vision to be absorbed by more participants.

Throughout this chapter I have included a mix of Visual, Auditory, and Kinesthetic words. A great exercise to help you get started on your journey is to reread this chapter and mark the margins with either V, A, or K each time you recognize one of these sensory words. This will allow your conscious mind to become more aware of these important descriptors. And just in case you read this chapter in a non-conscious state, this activity will help you succeed the second time around!

Stormie Andrews is licensed as a Practitioner of Neuro-Linguistics Programming by The Society of NLP. This chapter has been inspired by time tested NLP concepts.

Karl Schilling is President of Power Zone Training, providing sales coaching for small to mid-size businesses. He helps companies to increase revenues and profitability by letting the owners discover how to become decisive and take action – even if doing so involves calculated risks. Karl shares his unique style as a certified business coach and nationally-accredited sales trainer. He maintains a life-long commitment to the successful development of sales professionals and business owners.

Karl has more than 25 years in sales and sales training in both the financial services and real estate industries. Karl holds a Masters of Psychology and a Bachelor of Science degree in Business Administration. He is a published author, former College World Series coach, and former Major League Baseball scout. Contact Karl at 321-947-3220, *www.karlschilling.net* or e-mail him at *pzzone@aol.com.*

Chapter Twelve

"Failure is NOT a 4 – Letter Word!"

Karl Schilling

The concept of failure as a means to success is often ignored because most people identify failure with negative perceptions. To fully appreciate the benefits of failure, you must understand the *principles* of failure. These principles are:

Focus
Activity
Innovation
Learning
Urgency
Responsibility
Excellence

Notice that these principles spell "FAILURE"! Once you explore and understand each of these, you'll never look at failure the same way. In my book, *Fabulous Fortunes through F.A.I.L.U.R.E.*, and my presentation of the same name, I explore these principles in detail. Here is an introduction to them and their importance in your life.

Focus

The initial step is "Focus." Everything you are today is a direct result of your thinking patterns. It is your thinking that has driven you to the exact circumstances surrounding you right now! What has been your focus? Most people go through life without ever giving this a thought; the *idea* of focus is often overlooked and taken for granted. Your challenge is to get to the bottom of this initial principle. What do you want to do and how can you do it? Focus on the results you want to achieve and your pathway will become clear.

Activity

A powerful and clear focus will lead you to a certain level of activity. The illusion of security comes in the form of non-risk. When we marry up to this illusion, we create grave damage to ourselves. It is through this damage that we blame others and refuse to accept the basic accountability of our own inaction. In other words, the only true failure is *inaction*. This lack of action comes in many forms, but mostly through its most common form - procrastination. All roads in this condition lead to the same place: nowhere. Procrastination is firmly rooted in fear.

The value of failure can be difficult to recognize, especially in the midst of the failure. How can you come to grips with failure if you continually avoid it? You must move from avoidance and begin to embrace action. Your actions will bring about your results which can be good or bad.

Either way they can provide valuable lessons and move you closer to your goal. As a captain steers his ship, correcting for unexpected waves and currents, you too will need to make adjustments to your course to get where you're headed. Any kind of result is good, as it either takes you closer to your goal or shows you where a correction is needed. Earl Nightingale defined success as, "The progressive realization of a worthy goal or ideal." As long as you are moving toward your goal, you can consider yourself successful.

W. Clement Stone often spoke of the "seed of equivalent benefit." His belief was that in every defeat or dark circumstance there exists a positive benefit that can turn every defeat into future victory. I admit that this can be the most difficult thought process of all because it is asking you to find the good in some very negative situations.

Innovation
Your experience has now become valuable to you, whether it was a good or bad experience. Is it possible to lower the price of success? Yes; the new price is *innovation*. The process of innovation will create improved platforms on which you can develop your strategies. In

essence, you will be developing a new thought pattern. Exercising parts of your mind that have been sitting dormant means getting outside the box. You will have a refreshing new perception; people will begin to look different to you and they may react to you differently. That is because you *will be* different.

Conformity leads to mediocrity. You must take the time and energy to be innovative and tap in to your creativity, moving beyond conformity. Ignite your ambition and use that driving force - the hunger within you - to break out of the box and breathe the rarified air of success.

Learning
Learning is leverage for success. Another dependency belief is promulgated by the thought that *"I can't learn."* Countless people say this all the time... or that they are too timid to learn. How often have you heard the term *learning disability?* I submit there are no learning disabilities, only *teaching* disabilities. Every human being is a student of life. No one is disabled in the area of learning. You have already acquired an inordinate amount of knowledge that you are not consciously aware of.

In his marvelous book, "The Einstein Factor", Dr. Win Wenger shares that we are all genius laden. That's right; you are much brighter than you think. Every sound, sight, image, and concept that you've heard or seen since birth is loaded in your mind. Not one piece of information has been lost. The knowledge of how to retrieve it is the secret. The lessons you learned yesterday, along with the preparation you provide today, will create the future you will enjoy tomorrow!

The message here is about possibilities, not limitations. My goal is to reach and touch everyone I can to help them understand that we can each make a difference in the lives of others. While at times painful and frustrating, the overall impact of these lessons on my life has been exhilarating. I have learned that the great calling is to add value to others. Regardless of your occupation or calling in life, I know you have untapped value. Your opportunity for greatness lies in this resource. It is this value that you can share with others and make a difference in their lives.

Urgency

By forming a burning desire for what you want out of life you develop purpose.

We have discussed purpose in the form of a worthy ideal. It is in this ideal that your thoughts and beliefs become shaped and gain power. This creates a sense of urgency. The Japanese culture refers to this urgency symbolically as "having you hair on fire." Imagine the lengths you would go to put out a fire on your head! I dare say no time would be wasted and you would be highly motivated to resolve this issue.

So it is with your worthy ideal; define your urgency as such.

Responsibility

As urgency propels you toward achievement, you must take responsibility for your actions. We all share an individual responsibility to be accountable for our own thoughts. The great potential of mankind in is in the minds of each and every one of us. We have a moral, ethical, and social responsibility to continue our individual growth on a daily basis. Plus, it is through personal development and growth that we increase our value to each other. If you stop growing, you diminish your value to those around you. Everyone you come in contact with is cheated by your lack of growth. By undertaking your personal responsibility for self-improvement you are being responsible to the rest of society.

Excellence

Mastering failure will lead you to excellence. Taking responsibility leads you to mastery. Excellence is achieved through the use of your mind and will help you to reach the summit of success. As Aristotle so elegantly said, "We are what we repeatedly do; excellence, therefore, is not an act. It is a habit."

Using Failure to Assure Success

The course of action for tapping your unlimited resources is in F.A.I.L.U.R.E. **Focus** your energy on what you want in life. Take **action** and move toward this desire. Be **innovative** and creative by taking control of the masterpiece of your mind. Never stop **learning.** Pursue knowledge by learning the lessons of failure and mistakes. Be willing to take risks. Maintain the sense of **urgency** necessary to propel you toward the success you desire. Take **responsibility** for identifying your worthy ideal. Be responsible and accountable for your goals and delivering value to others. Lastly, establish the **excellence** that will formulate your platform, enabling you to make a difference in people's lives.

Dr. Caroline Williams is a successful Chiropractor, philosopher, teacher and entrepreneur.

She has been helping patients and clients optimize their health for more than ten years. Her focus has always been on empowering and coaching her patients. Her motto, "Invest in your health to win," sets her apart from her peers. She utilizes the same, fundamental principles that successful people use to create wealth to help her patients in promoting optimal health.

Her experience as a successful fitness competitor taught her the power of focus, commitment and hard work. She especially enjoys sharing her secrets to health and wealth with direct marketing companies and specializes in women's groups.

To contact Dr Caroline Williams, call 702-938-0199 or visit her website at *www.investinyourhealthtowin.com.*

Chapter Thirteen

Purpose + Philosophy = Success

Dr. Caroline Williams

Is it easier to succeed when you are engaged in your passion? How can you determine where your passion lies and how can you connect with it? And, does greater understanding of your passion, motivation and your internal guidance system help you to achieve greater success in *every* aspect of your life?

For years, people have been asking these questions, and I'm no exception! What is it that makes some people tremendously successful while others struggle just to survive? I grew up with a natural, built-in desire to want to be the best I could possibly be... at everything I did. I was always athletic and competitive, which is why I was quick to notice the difference between athletes. I wondered about the differences that make some athletes simply good while others become truly great.

A Heartfelt Decision

I began my quest to answer this by researching the best training routines and supplements to enhance my own athletic performance. I did the research and applied all that I learned. This was at a time in my life when I was trying to figure out what profession I wanted to pursue. The most logical choice was to engage in a career where I could apply my passion for physical excellence and enhanced performance. I struggled with my decision about whether I should go into Chiropractic or Physical Therapy (which my family preferred) and, after comparing the two programs, I chose Chiropractic. I wanted to work with others who were committed to excellence.

This decision did not earn the blessings of my family; in fact they were extremely discouraging about it. They didn't have the same outlook that I did regarding alternative medicine, and they were more influenced by public perception than I was. I was more influenced by my heart and passion for what I wanted to do. Everything else was just details.

How is this relevant to *your* success? I discovered that when you are passionate about what you do, it doesn't seem like work. Plus, you attract support and interest because others find your enthusiasm contagious. The passion you feel drives you forward and catapults you to success. Think of passion as "love on fire."

The energy that is generated by intense love of something is extremely powerful.

Success actually begins in the nonphysical realm. It starts out as an idea or a thought, but that is not enough to manifest it in the physical realm. You also need emotion behind the idea. It is the emotion that gives the idea the energy and drive it needs to manifest. The final step is following through and acting on this idea. When you take action, you bring this creation into the physical realm. Your action is the confirmation of your intention and desire.

Thinking, Feeling, and Acting
All three components - thinking, feeling, and acting - are necessary to achieve success, and all three need to be in alignment. The thing that struck me about Chiropractic and why I chose it was that it had a philosophy that was in alignment with my own. It was no coincidence that my favorite subject in undergrad school was Philosophy. I felt passionately about Chiropractic and the philosophy behind it and was able to act on that passion. I was pursuing it and it never felt like work. Everything was in alignment.

Why is it so important to have a philosophy? It is the foundation for all your ideas about the world and your place in it. And it allows you to think in terms of concepts. Your philosophy influences your ideas and the choices you make, whether you are consciously aware of it or not.

This is why, when I educate my patients, I focus on teaching a concept which could be applied to any scenario. In this way, I empower them to think for themselves rather than to rely on me for all the answers. You've no doubt heard the expression, "Give a man a fish and he will eat for a day; *teach* a man to fish and he will eat for a lifetime." I am fulfilling my purpose knowing that I am educating my patients to improve their own lives.

Helping Patients to Help Themselves

My methodology can be challenging at times because so many people are used to going to their doctors and simply being told what to do - without any explanation. I've often heard my patients say, "Doctor Williams, just tell me what to do." Of course I could do that, but without an understanding of *why* I am recommending a certain course of action or treatment, my patients won't necessarily stick with it. The odds of them adhering to any program for their entire lifetime increase once they understand the philosophy behind my advice. How does this impact their level of success? Understanding the various concepts empowers them; they then have a basis on which to make a choice and, most importantly, a choice that will serve them versus one that does not.

It's important to understand that wherever there is a problem, a solution exists as well. This is supported by the fact that we live in a world of duality; Yin and Yang energy, good and bad, and so on. A problem and a solution are two sides of the same coin.

When a problem lies within a person, so does the solution. If we are equipped with the ability to ask ourselves the right questions, the solution will present itself. By learning how to solve our own problems, we will also become better at preventing them, too. You can see how this translates into developing greater wisdom and the evolution of consciousness. This greater level of awareness is what we are.

Divine Intelligence
The philosophy of Chiropractic is one that recognizes and acknowledges the innate intelligence that we all possess. Another way to look at it is to recognize how divine intelligence takes care of the functions of our bodies without us ever having to think about it. Imagine if you had to consciously tell your heart to beat every time or tell your lungs to expand and contract with each and every breath, or for our immune system to respond when we breathe polluted air and it automatically protects us from unseen toxins. Our divine intelligence is what ensures our survival. It is easy to take this for granted, but it is what allows us to have the freedom to consciously create. Without this

subconscious intelligence we would never have time for anything else.

Divine intelligence is also our intuition. I'm sure you've experienced a "gut feeling" that told you something was wrong or guided you in making a right decision. That is your internal guidance system. Understanding and listening to your internal guidance system is key to one's success. This has also been referred to as Emotional Intelligence.

We all have different ideas about what it means to be successful, and for most of us, that idea that is continually changing and evolving. It comes down to the ability to choose what you want in life and then being able to manifest it. What you begin to realize is that it is not the end result that makes us happy as most of us beginning a new journey may think. It's the actual journey and the pursuit of our dreams that generates the greatest feelings of happiness and success.

A Goal Achieved is No Longer a Goal

That's why when someone sets a goal for themselves and they finally achieve it, they don't just stop there. They reassess and create new goals and dreams. The fundamental truth is that we need and want to fulfill our purpose. It is in the pursuit and fulfillment of our purpose that we develop and recognize our self worth. Our internal guidance is there to help us find our purpose. We are able to recognize it by connecting with our passion for it – just as I connected with Chiropractic and the study of philosophy. The challenge for many of us is in choosing to acknowledge that passion and nurture it - even in the face of discouragement.

In my quest for physical excellence and performance, I discovered that it wasn't just the physical attributes that made an athlete great as I had thought in the beginning. It was the strength of their human spirit that made the ultimate difference.

Michelle Johnson Littleton, founder of Diva Las Vegas Productions, is a multi-lingual, top-rated consultant and entertainment producer for high profile corporate clients and celebrities worldwide.

Michelle has a degree in English Language and Literature from Yale University. She is an accomplished world class performer who has performed on Broadway and toured or recorded with such artists as Gladys Knight, Sheena Easton, Sugarland, and Elton John.

Michelle is a member of the National Association of Women Business Owners and is an active advocate for women in business. As a mentor, she helps women who are seeking careers in entertainment, production, and public speaking. Michelle's forthcoming book, *The Chick Singer Bible*, delves into vital skills for women in business, including some rarely discussed pitfalls in the music business. Catch her newsletter for aspiring female musicians at *www.chicksingerbible.com.* Visit Michelle at *www.divalasvegas.com*, e-mail *info@ divalasvegas.com* or call 702-385-3482.

Chapter Fourteen
The Pivotal Moment ... 20 Years Ago
Michelle Littleton

Pivotal: vitally important: CRITICAL

I had been preparing for weeks for my first concert of original music. I was excited and completely wrapped up in all of the publicity and buzz that had been generated for the event. My wardrobe was selected and my hair was done. I was a successful New York City vocalist who had toured and recorded as a backup singer for major artists, and this would be my first large solo show. I was taking a big step by agreeing to sing my own music at a local music festival in front of 10,000 people, the largest crowd I had serenaded to date. I was nervous, but as those in the music business would say, it was a "good nervous."

I had handpicked the best musicians in town to back me up on stage. These musicians were my dearest friends with whom I'd collaborated on many projects over the years. Nothing could go wrong, I thought.

What happened next would come to define how I look at life, relationships, work, and accountability.

Out of Tune
That afternoon, I held a rehearsal at my home. I had a great rapport with these friends who were now working for me. I confidently placed my charts – my prized sheets of music – in front of them and we began to play. I started to sing my heart out.

Suddenly, the band stopped. "What part are you on?" "Where do we go after that section?" We resumed playing only to fall apart repeatedly. "What key are we in now?" "This doesn't make any sense." The questions were directed to each other, as if I were not even there. The more I attempted to answer the barrage of questions, the more my friends tuned me out. I felt invisible. It was like nothing I had ever experienced.

One by one, my friends turned on me, now with full-blown anger. "You aren't prepared." "You have no idea what you are doing." "You are wasting our time." Then, they started walking out. Rehearsal was over.

Understanding the Real Problem
I was surprised and shocked. I did not understand the problem. The music made

sense to me. I knew exactly what I wanted. Demoralized, embarrassed, and heartbroken, I was at a complete loss.

The final two band members, women, stayed behind to make sure I was alright. One of them said, "Michelle, you are a good musician and a great singer, but you are the only one who knows how to play your music. Your charts are a mess and they don't make any sense. You just don't speak our language."

The other musician chimed in. "It's about respect. You expect us to come to you and make you sound great, but you don't respect the tools we use to do that. A chart of music is a map that shows us where to go and how to get there. It needs to be consistent so that we all end up in the same place. Musicians go to great lengths to study theory and basic music lingo, but singers expect us to be mind readers. It's rude and unprofessional. That is why your friends just walked out. Learn our language or hire someone else who does. You need a music director. We'd help you if you would have simply asked."

What Your Friends Won't Tell You
My head opened up as their words struck my ears. What they were saying made perfect sense to me. I wondered how long this frustration had been brewing. My first reaction though, was "Why didn't anyone just tell me?"

I was blessed by the compassionate intervention of these two friends. They stayed late into the night, giving me a crash course in all things musical as they pertain to musicians reading music. They took the time to rewrite my charts and showed me how and why I needed to do certain things for my career as a composer, performer, and colleague.

The next day all of the music read perfectly. To my relief, the concert was both a personal and professional success. More importantly, I learned valuable lessons that continue to shape my paradigms and help me to help others as I pay forward the incredible acts of kindness and compassion that were bestowed upon me that day.

We can learn something every day, but *how* and *where* we learn is as crucial to a lesson's impact as *what* we learn. Most of us harbor insecurities in a least a few areas, so we tend to stay in our comfort zones. We don't like being criticized so we don't seek outside opinions about what we are doing and how we are doing it. We want to feel good about ourselves.

Removing Self-Limiting Behaviors

In our *everyday behaviors*, we not only fail to recognize certain characteristics as self-limiting, but we actually *cling* to them fiercely because we believe they are working well for us. Despite weaknesses in some areas, we can still say "I excel at networking" or "My presentation skills are great; it's my marketing I need to work on" or "I communicate well and people trust me; at least that isn't an issue." We tend not to see the negative aspects of our behavior.

Look at my story. I spoke several languages and had traveled the world playing music. I consistently received positive reviews. I'd played Broadway and even Carnegie Hall. People everywhere loved my singing and asked for my records. I was a confident Ivy League graduate. On a personal level, I was popular... the "go to" person for all of my friends. Confident that my game plan was solid, I naturally concluded that I was on the right track. I was a great communicator. Musicians and fans alike adored me. I was a consummate pro.

So, personally AND professionally, I felt pretty good about myself. It took something professionally catastrophic to turn my thinking upside down. I had to re-learn who I was through the eyes of other people... people I loved and trusted. People who loved me enough to tell me off. I had stopped paying attention to what and who was right in front of me. I had bought into my own hype... I "believed my own press."

You can move through the rest of your life without ever seeing yourself and your patterns for what they are. Many "successful" people do just that. These behaviors and belief systems can be self-imposed road blocks, carefully camouflaged as well-developed skills and paradigms, that actually keep us from growing.

Being Willing to Change

Now I am not suggesting that you panic and abandon everything that you feel good about. Loving yourself is the key to any form of success. But be willing to pivot away from your comfort zone. It's not that scary; when you pivot, one foot stays grounded as you focus on your goal. You are just turning away from your old point of view to see if there is a better vantage point... a new opportunity. You are pivoting away from your *basic assumptions* about what is working for you, and what makes you feel safe and secure. You are taking a chance.

This requires courage, strength, and a willingness to ask for help. My wonderful friends showed me that I didn't know I needed help or how to ask for it. Having to ask for help was an underlying fear that had kept me from doing so many things. I was afraid to "lose myself" and change those things that I believed I did well. I had become overly confident and intimidating to others, which made me unapproachable.

I thought I "played well with others," but when my core beliefs were challenged, it was obvious that I didn't. I had also ignored other instances of effective band leading that I had seen in action and concluded that I had "my own style" and it worked for me. And to think... all I had to do was learn to write a decent chart.

116

That was my pivotal moment. It changed the way I work with musicians and business people. It forced me to really learn my craft as a complete musician, not just a performer. Eventually, it allowed me to become a sought after music director and event producer.

As a producer, I work for and with people in countless professions and I have learned to speak all of their "languages." Here in Las Vegas and across the globe, I am equally comfortable with celebrities or the housekeeping staff. In some ways, I am a walking, talking chameleon, having become very adaptable to all situations. Nonetheless, I maintain core beliefs and values that sustain me in every business relationship.

Today I am passionate about giving back to aspiring, young entertainers by sharing my stories of personal development, change, and growth. In that spirit, I am currently writing a funny, instructional book called *The Chick Singer Bible.*

If you have an interest in the music industry or in business development for women, you can sign up for my newsletter at *www.chicksingerbible.com.*

Yasmine Bijan is a passionate and inspirational motivational speaker, certified coach, and transformational business leader in the areas of self-empowerment, interpersonal communication, and business leadership. Yasmine draws upon her background in sales and marketing, management, and training for a Fortune 500 wireless company. Her presentations are especially targeted to technology and the financial services industry, as well as to general audiences where her knowledge of business relationships and leadership has inspired thousands to live extraordinary lives.

She recently was featured as a *Master Mentor* in the insightful documentary films *The Power of Mentorship: the Movie* and *The Voices of Women.* She is also a contributing author to several books such as *The Power of Coaching II,* and *The Power of Mentorship: The Law of Attraction, Special Edition.* She was also a finalist for the *2007 San Diego Business Journal's "Women Who Mean Business" Award.*

You can visit her at *www.YasmineBijan.com* or join Yasmine's professional online networking community at *www.HeartNetworking.com.* E-mail Yasmine at *Yasmine@YasmineBijan.com* or call 858-922-5350.

Chapter Fifteen

Step Up and Step Into the Leader Within

Yasmine Bijan

Have you wanted to contribute more, be more, love more, or connect more with others? Do you want to let your light shine brightly, but don't know how to do it, or are afraid of what might happen if you do? Have you ever asked yourself "Is this all there is?"

I certainly have had those thoughts and experiences throughout my life. In fact, my life has been a journey to discover the elusive answers to the deepest questions that plague many of us. It's because of this journey that I am now able to share my experience with you.

What to Do When You Are NOT a Born Leader
I have often asked myself, "How can I further tap into my own greatest gifts, talents, and passions and share them with the world?" The answer I found was so simple. I realized that when I stepped up, stepped outside of my

comfort zone, and connected with people that I was ultimately stepping into the leader within. By stepping into my power, I could become a beacon of light for others. But how did a shy, little girl become a leader? Experience!

For me, leadership wasn't a natural born gift, skill, or talent, but rather, something that I had committed to developing. Like many people, I believed that I had to be born with an outgoing, perhaps even boisterous or domineering personality to be a considered an effective leader. The truth is that leadership shows up in many ways; it is a learnable skill. With tenacity and courage, anyone can be a leader. You just need someone to show you how to tap in to the leader within you.

Everyone in my family – except me – was boisterous and expressive; I was extremely quiet and shy. In fact, I wondered if I was adopted and they just didn't want to tell me. My father was a world-renowned creative genius; my mother was a brilliant business woman; my sister was an outgoing actress; and my brother was the youngest and the cutest. I dreaded when strangers would try to talk with me. I was horrified if someone in the grocery line acknowledged me, or tried to ask me a question. I hid behind my mom and clung to her leg for dear life!

As I grew older, I didn't think I had much to say or contribute. I was insecure and I wasn't good at self-expression. I was terrified to share my thoughts for fear of what people might think. I compensated by becoming a "People-Pleasing Accommodator." I'm sure you know the type! I had found solace in reading my Nancy Drew and Hardy Boys novels while snuggling up with my tiny white poodle, "Buttons." I would sit comfortably in the privacy of my own room, escaping into adventures I never dreamed I would ever experience in "real life." Occasionally, however, the daredevil in me would manage to shine through. I was a roller-skating queen rolling to the music of Abba, skating up and down steep hills. I enjoyed playing in the street with the neighborhood kids. When playing, I didn't have to talk much.

I began to step outside my comfort zone and I learned to connect with people. When I was a freshman in high school, my family relocated from our fast-paced city life to a rural area. They bought a 20-acre property that seemed to be in the middle of nowhere. I was about to embark on a huge adventure. I had to create a new life for myself. That thought horrified me, but moving to a new city somehow forced me to drop any limiting perceptions of myself and reinvent a new, more capable me.

I continued to step up and step out. Riding the bus forced me into conversations with my classmates. I met my best friend on that bus. Sharing a seat on the bus was a fairly safe way to start a conversation or make new friends.

Before long, I became a social butterfly – at least when it was just one-on-one. I would simply ask questions and do a lot of listening. I still wasn't sure if I had anything important to say, and I didn't like being the center of attention. I eventually mustered up the courage to get involved in group activities. I found myself attending more events and even started going to group dances. By my junior year, I joined the tennis team and had even signed up for drama class. Being active, just as when playing with kids on the street, made socializing much easier!

Practice Makes Perfect

With more practice, it eventually became effortless to connect, relate, and be with people. When one-on-one with people, I put the focus on them. When passing people in the hallway, I would smile, look them in the eye and say "Hello." In conversations, I wanted to learn more about who they were and what motivated them. I was a good listener. What I found most surprising was that people would respond and say "Wow, Yasmine, you are so great!" I hadn't quite figured out why they thought that of me because I didn't ever say much in those conversations. Later, I realized that people appreciated the gift that my attentive listening provided. They enjoyed my attention and encouragement. My active listening made them feel appreciated and acknowledged.

By the time I was a senior in high school, I was on the yearbook staff, interviewing students and teachers alike. So much for being shy! I made so many friends, all from various backgrounds. I was dating the high school quarterback and later became Senior Prom Queen. The day after the prom, my best friend called me at work, screaming for me to get that day's copy of *The Sacramento Bee*. A local photographer had submitted a picture of me and there it was - on the front page of the largest newspaper in the area! It had bold captions describing who I was, what I was about, and utilized my story as an example to illustrate the role of "Senior Prom Queen."

Whether or not I was ready for it, I realized my light was shining brighter than ever before. I was inspiring and influencing many people. I realized that by getting involved, connecting and caring about people, stepping outside my comfort zone, and having the courage to take risks, I was allowing my leader within to shine. I had actually become a role model for others!

Throughout college, I stepped out and explored more of my passions, gifts, and talents. I wanted to discover how I could contribute more, be more, love more, and connect more. I took a bold step and registered for a Bachelor's Degree in Communications (of all things!) My family didn't understand what a communications degree was, but by that time, I no longer cared about what others thought. I was on a mission! I joined the speech and debate team, became the communications student body president, was an ambassador and orientation leader for my university, studied abroad in England, back-packed through Europe for six weeks, and was an apprentice intern news reporter at a local television station. I was living adventures that I had only read about; now I rivaled Nancy Drew's experience!

After graduating, I began what would become a 12-year career with one of the most recognizable brands in wireless communication. Throughout my career I realized that the leadership qualities and skills I had developed in high school and college transferred well into the fields of sales, marketing, training, and management.

Following my passion, I continued to participate in programs that fostered my personal, professional, and humanitarian development. I still find solace in reading books, (mostly in the area of personal and professional development), and snuggling with my furry little Pomeranian, Kiya. I continue to travel throughout America and abroad. By tapping into my leadership skills and by becoming involved, I found myself.

Today, I own a transformational business leadership consulting and training firm called InPowerU. My education and experience, along with the challenges that I have overcome, have enabled me to help other people discover the joys of tapping into their own greatest gifts, talents, and passions. When we get involved in making a difference in the lives of others, it's easier for us to transform our own self-limiting perceptions about who we are and what we are truly capable of achieving. Getting involved helps us to discover what's possible.

Discovering increased ways to shine my own light enables me to light the way for others - in both business and in life. Through my coaching and mentoring programs, I am now able to share my experiences, wisdom, gifts, talents, and passions to help others. I get to share through live events as well as through audio, DVD, and books. I am passionate about helping others to ignite their leader within. My goal is to help people expedite their success and achieve their greatest dreams and desires. With tenacity, courage, and someone to show you how, you can learn to be the leader you desire to be. It is available within us all! For more information, visit *www.YasmineBijan. com.*

Dale Halaway inspires and empowers organizations and individuals to bring about positive, lasting change. He has been helping people transform their lives for more than thirty years. The success stories from his students and corporate clients are a testimony to the impact Dale has had in their personal and professional lives.

Dale is the president and CEO of Inspiring Seminars, LLC. His work as an international speaker, transformational teacher, master sales trainer and life coach has inspired thousands of entrepreneurs, sales professionals, businesses and leaders of all types to dramatically improve their personal effectiveness and productivity levels.

For more information on Dale Halaway or to see the impact he's had on his clients, visit *www.EmpoweredSelling.com* and *www. SeminarsThatInspire.com.* For keynotes or interactive transformational workshops for your meeting or conference, email Dale at *DHInspires@aol.com* or call him directly at 702-860-6144.

Chapter Sixteen

Discovering Your Soul's Purpose

Dale Halaway

For those of you who have chosen to live an enlightened life, connecting with your higher self can be challenging at times. Being "in alignment" with our higher self actually means being in alignment with our soul's purpose.

The Struggle to Find Our Purpose

Many people struggle in their search to find their purpose. They wander from job to job or start up one business after another, never quite clicking with anything. Some continue to keep a business or career going long after it's become obvious that it is no longer working. Even though their work or business may be noble and serving, the universe is trying to show them it isn't in alignment with their true purpose.

Negativity

There are three specific things that can block us from realizing our soul's purpose. *The first is negativity.* As humans, we tend to hold on to negative thoughts and emotions until we become aware of them and then choose to let them go. Whether we use EFT (Emotional Freedom Technique) or TLC (Transformational Life Coaching System, a method which I developed and teach in my seminars), one of the key steps in transforming or letting go of this negative energy is to acknowledge it by giving it a clear voice.

We have core negative emotions, including jealousy, insecurity, guilt, resentment, fear and anger. When we hold on to these emotions, they are stored in the physical or subconscious body. These negative emotions, if not released and dealt with correctly, attract even more negativity, weighing us down until it begins to feel like we are sinking in quicksand.

This negative energy blocks the flow of positive energy – your higher self – the part of you that is your power, your strength, your creativity, your wisdom – your *real* self! When we bring our personal and professional lives into alignment with our real self, we feel inspired, connected, loved and protected.

By holding on to negative emotions, we remain separate from the issues we need to deal with. It's as though these issues don't exist, when in fact they really do. No matter how much we may engage in behaviors to mask or cover up these emotions, they are with us wherever we go. Negative energy generates more negative energy, either in our physical bodies or in other aspects of our physical life. Because all energy is in a constant state of motion, no one can stop it from moving. In other words, we cannot escape from our negativity. The truth is we must deal with it through acceptance and by understanding its purpose; only then can we let it go.

It takes a great deal of our energy to resist or avoid these negative emotions. This can be very tiring. Most of us are probably not even aware that we are resisting. Those who are in resistance and avoidance usually have a behavioral pattern of pushing. This constant pushing is what makes people feel burned out; they are constantly pushing to get projects done or pushing others to comply and conform. Once we let go of resisting the negative and learn how to correctly work with this energy, we become able to connect with the positive energy that lies underneath all of the negative energy. Blocked negative energy also blocks our positive energy behind it.

Instead of denying or suppressing our own negativity and negative emotions, we need to learn how to release this energy from our subconscious. In many cases, part of our soul's purpose actually lies in our need to clear out this negative energy. It's the urging of one's soul or higher self that causes all growth.

Learning how to do this "inner work" helps us on the path to discovering our unique purpose. Because this inner work has to do with facing parts of ourselves that we don't want to see or that we're afraid of, it's best to have a counselor, teacher or life coach guide us through whatever transformational process they use in assisting their clients to heal their subconscious bodies. Rather than always trying to control everything, I recommend the daily practice of self-inquiry, meditation and journaling, as these processes can help to slow us down and relax into our thoughts and feelings.

Life really begins once our souls get their own way with us. Imagine what it would be like to no longer be affected by what others are doing or saying! This is emotional mastery; being emotionally clear, secure and stable. You are now the embodiment of your higher self. By engaging in good quality inner work and turning the spiritual discipline of consciously releasing our negative energy through healthy and empowering methods, we discover how to master these emotions.

Judgment

The second thing that blocks us from discovering our soul's purpose is judgment. Have you noticed how some people are so quick to judge, yet so slow to change their *own* ways? Some act as if they were given a license to be judge and jury. The truth is they weren't. Dr. Wayne Dyer said, "Judging someone as stupid doesn't mean they're stupid. It means... you are defining them as stupid!" Those who live in judgment are the ones who end up paying the price. When somebody is judging, they really have some part of themselves in judgment and probably aren't even conscious of it. When someone is free from their own judgment, they will no longer judge others; they will naturally allow everyone in their world to be exactly who they are.

Judgment creates a separation or division which keeps people from being in alignment with their higher self. What's interesting is that the universe does not judge us. Judgment is something we as people have created. Once we are in judgment, we are no longer in the flow of life.

If authentic leadership in business or any environment is really about setting a powerful and positive example for those around us, how does it help to continue down this path of holding others in judgment? It doesn't! What most people don't realize is that the very thing we judge in others actually becomes locked into place and strengthens. How many of us have made statements like, "I'd never do what they do." or "I'll never become like them." Then, at some later point in life we realize that we are becoming the very person we said we would never become. We usually judge others on those things that we dislike about ourselves. It's just easier to see this behavior in others.

The opposite of judgment is a state of total and complete acceptance. Love transcends and melts judgment. Wherever there is judgment there can be no love. Wherever there is unconditional love, judgment cannot exist for any length of time. This is exactly what we are here to learn – how to love more and judge less. There is a beautiful, yet simple Sioux Indian prayer we can use: "Great Spirit, help me never to judge another until I have walked in his moccasins for two weeks."

Imbalance

The third thing is imbalance. Within us we have masculine and feminine energy, or yin/ yang energy. When these two energies are not in harmony with each other, an imbalance occurs. This simply means that there is conflict between these two significant parts of ourselves. Negative energy is being held very tightly in the subconscious body, creating resistance. This can be very painful. One part is getting more energy than the other and one part feels judged for causing this imbalance. The latter part is living in this energy of judgment, which means it's locked in a dark place. It's not allowed to come into the light and be acknowledged.

Most men and women today are leading their lives more with their masculine energy and are suppressing their feminine energy, which can create a lot of pain. Because the feminine energy is the receiving side of us, this can also create an experiential effect in our lives which can manifest into the lack of money, lack of time and/or lack of love. This imbalance can also manifest in the business world when employees are placed improperly in positions where their strengths are not being realized.

How do we become balanced? First, we must learn to become aware of our resistance so that we can let go of whoever or whatever we're resisting. Then, once we are aware of it, we can purge and let go of all the negative material that's been trapped within the subconscious body once and for all.

We will all eventually discover this truth: regardless of how challenging our lives can be, our saving grace will be found in the real cellular healing of our subconscious body. Healing our subconscious body sets us free from all our negativity and judgment, and it brings us back into balance. If one person can do it... everyone can. Realize your true potential and purpose, not through the process of trying to figure it out in your head, but by releasing the negativity that you have been holding on to in your subconscious body. The way to your higher self and your soul's purpose is through your lower self... the subconscious self!

Judi Moreo talks about success and she lives it! In 1992, she became the first female executive in one of South Africa's most prestigious media groups during times of turmoil and unrest. In 2003, the U.S. Business Advisory Council named her "Nevada Business Person of the Year" and the Las Vegas Chamber of Commerce presented her company, Turning Point International, with a "Circle of Excellence" award.

Judi is the author of *You Are More Than Enough: Every Woman's Guide to Purpose, Passion, and Power,* and is co-author of *Conquer the Brain Drain: 52 Creative Ways to Pump Up Productivity, Ordinary Women, Extraordinary Success,* and *Getting Things Done.* Visit Judi at *www.JudiMoreo.com,* e-mail *JudiMoreo@Yahoo. com* or call 702-896-2228.

Chapter Seventeen

Discipline: The Key to Success

Judi Moreo

Discipline is a major key to success. It is the ability to do what needs to be done at the appropriate time in order to accomplish your desired goals.

Taking The First Step

My friend Wally, who is 72-years old, runs three miles every weekday morning and has done so for 35 years. He is in excellent health and looks like he is 55 years old. I asked him how he manages to get up every weekday morning and go out to run no matter what the weather. Wally answered simply, "I put my running shoes on." I'd say that's the first step, as well as the perfect metaphor for starting and then following through on any goal.

To be disciplined, you must consistently take the first step toward whatever it is that you want to achieve. Make a decision to do something and then do what has to be done; follow through until you achieve your goal.

What do you need to do to make your dreams come true? First, you must decide what it is that you want. Be specific; set a goal and devise a plan to achieve it. Then, as my friend Wally says, "Put on your running shoes!" Simply take the first step. After that, take another... and another.

Breaking it Down

Sometimes, we become overwhelmed if we think about accomplishing an entire project or achieving a lofty goal instead of taking it one step at a time. If your goal is to write a book, you don't sit down and write an entire book at once! You start by writing a page at a time. If you want to build a house, you first must come up with a plan and the design for it. Then, you lay the foundation. So it is with any goal; take that first step and before you know it, you'll be well on your way.

With self-discipline, you can rid yourself of bad habits, overcome addictions, eliminate procrastination, and create order where there once was chaos. Discipline is the creation of good habits. It's always easier to take the path of non-resistance. That's where discipline comes in. When you do what you don't necessarily feel like doing at the time, focusing more on your ultimate goal, you create good habits that ultimately make your life easier.

Self-discipline has to be developed. Science has proven that it takes twenty-one days to establish new patterns or habits. Look at the overall picture of your life... career, finances, relationships, health, community involvement, spiritual practices, recreation, and education. Do you have what you want in each of these areas of your life? If not, start by setting some goals. Do something each day to make your life better. Don't set too many goals or try to do too much at one time. Choose one area and take the necessary steps. When you are doing well in that area, move to the next. Continue to do this until you have created the habits you need to make your life more ideal!

The greater your self-discipline, the easier it will become. It builds upon itself. The more you do, the more you get. Associate with others who are disciplined. Some of it will rub off on you.

Perhaps your goal is to do more to advance your career. Start by examining how you spend your time. Are you busy doing unproductive work? Ask yourself, "Is this helping me to accomplish my goal?" Every step you take and every decision you make should be in complete harmony with what you are doing and what you hope to achieve. Discipline yourself to consistently make the right decisions. Creating the right habits will ultimately move you closer to your dreams.

Marcia Wieder, America's Dream Coach®, has helped thousands of people worldwide achieve their personal and professional dreams. To receive a free *Jumpstart Your Dream* kit and discover information on Marcia's programs and global community, "Amazing Dreamers," go to *www.dreamcoach.com*.

In addition to being a charismatic speaker, she's the renowned author of four books dedicated to achieving your dreams: *Making Your Dreams Come True®, Life is But a Dream, Dreams are Whispers From the Soul* and *Doing Less and Having More.* She's also a syndicated columnist for The San Francisco Chronicle. Marcia founded Dream University, where she has certified close to 1000 Dream Coaches to lead her masterful work. Contact Marcia at 415-381-5564 or *info@dreamcoach.com*.

Chapter Eighteen

Six Serious Fear Busters

Marcia Wieder

Seen on a tip jar in a coffee shop:
"If you fear change, leave it here."

Do you dream of a life where you have impact, contribute to the well-being of others, and maintain a certain lifestyle? As you get closer to fulfilling this dream (or any other dream you have), doubt and fear may surface. There are simple and practical steps you can take to get rid of these evils.

The number one way we sabotage our dreams is by saying things like, "But, what if?" and imagining the worst. But, what if I...

- Fail?
- Succeed?
- Say or do the wrong thing?
- Don't know the answer?
- Don't get enough clients?
- Don't make enough money?

Often, irrational thoughts attack our rational minds. We invent terrifying tales that magnify our fears. When you start to wonder, "But, what if?", you are caught in the common pattern of projecting fear and doubt into your dream. With this thinking, as you move toward your dream, you'll also move toward your fears and worst nightmares. What we focus on grows, whether it is fear and doubt or achieving our dreams. Our fears can take hold, which is why most of us give up - or never even begin.

1. If you feel afraid or indecisive, this simple exercise can help you stabilize. Draw a line across the center of a paper. On the top, write your dream in as much detail as possible. On the bottom, write out your reality (about this dream) including your fears, doubts and "but, what ifs". Are you more committed to your dream or to your fear?

Two things will cause you to be more committed to your fear. The first is if you don't have a clearly defined dream. The second is if you project your worst fears into your dream. When fear is placed in its proper place, as part of reality, it is easier to be more committed to your vision... and fear simply becomes something to manage.

2. As you connect to your dreams or at different intervals along your path, you'll often run into the voice of your "Doubter." We either ignore or obsess over this aspect, because it

tells us everything that might go wrong. Left unattended, this voice can be disruptive. But turn the Doubter down and it becomes the voice of the "Realist," who primarily wants to know what you are planning, usually related to time and money issues. Early on, you may not have all the details figured out, so going to strategy too soon can actually hinder or limit your dream.

Interview your Doubter and be curious. Capture its needs, insights, and wisdom by completing these sentences (multiple times):

"The way I sabotage _____'s (your name) dream is _____."

Example: "The way I sabotage Jenny's dream is by having her doubt herself and quit."

"When I am running _____'s (your name) life, I _____."

Example: "When I am running Jenny's life, I keep her too busy to focus on what's important."

"What I need from _____ (your name) is _____."

Example: "What I need from Jenny is for her to have faith, to get help, to breathe."

3. Your Doubter can provide a list of obstacles based on its fears and concerns, which are either involve limiting beliefs (an internal job) or require a plan (an external job). Some obstacles

may be both and they can be real or imagined. The Dream Coach® rule is "Wherever there's an obstacle, design a strategy to manage it." Make a list of your obstacles and identify which ones are negative self-perceptions or beliefs and which ones require strategies.

Obstacles List for Your Dream (Examples)

- I don't know how. (belief and strategy)
- I'm afraid I will fail. (belief)
- I don't have the money. (strategy)
- I'm too tired. (belief and strategy)

The first step in managing fear is to identify exactly what you are afraid if. Just saying, "I'm afraid," can be a whitewash and can keep you stuck. Identify what you fear. For example, if you are afraid you can't make a good living doing what you love, explore ways to check out your assumptions or to get training.

Sometimes there is no evidence that this is the right time to pursue your dream, especially if you focus on your fear - or even some aspects of reality. Don't look in your checkbook, the stock market, or in the approval of others for evidence of whether or not you should be afraid or believe in your dream. The place to look is in your own heart. Can you believe in something because it matters to you and demonstrate that you believe in it by taking action? This is where powerful breakthroughs occur.

4. Here's a critical and proven point: Beliefs are never neutral. They either move you forward or hold you back. But, you choose what to believe. The way to move from limiting beliefs that hold you back to empowering beliefs that move you forward is through willingness, courage, and practice. Be willing to believe in yourself and your dreams and have the courage to act on what you believe. Develop this as part of your identity by practicing this behavior continuously until it becomes true.

5. Are you aware of what typically stops you? For most of us, it has to do with something we hate, we're not good at, or that we have no idea how to tackle. It can be frightening, and when *that* task is essential to the success of your venture, it could be your demise. Don't allow one need or issue to destroy your dream. Here are some options:

- Identify the block or area of concern.
- Decide if you are going to tackle it yourself.
- If not, find someone who can do it with or for you.
- Hire them or trade for something they need.
- Get back into action on the areas where you excel.

If your dream is to write a book but you can't type or are computer-phobic, this doesn't have to stop you. Learn a new skill or hire someone.

If you can't afford that, explore bartering. If you are branching out into a new area and lack knowledge or experience, educating yourself is essential. Does it make more sense to take a class or would it be faster and easier to find a mentor? Get creative and get going. The time you waste worrying would best be used seeking guidance and finding answers.

6. Overcome fear and other obstacles (even time and money issues) by enrolling others into your vision. Master this skill and you'll accomplish bigger dreams with less effort. One of the most powerful ways to overcome the fear of not having clients or making enough money is to be able to talk to anyone, anytime, and anyplace about their dreams in a way where *they* feel inspired. Ask what their personal or professional dreams are and explore how you can help them achieve what they want. Build enough value and the objection around cost often disappears. Here are the key steps:

- Establish rapport and relationship
- Build value by asking good questions.
- Overcome objections by revisiting steps #1 and 2.
- Secure an agreement by negotiating as needed. It could be for a meeting, a complimentary session, or to begin your new venture. If people say no, be courageous and ask why. Make specific requests that make it easy for others to say yes.

Build an arsenal of winning behaviors and people that you can reach out to in a pinch. There is nothing worse than feeling desperate and having no place to turn. Develop a robust database of brilliant resources that you can access at any given moment. Build a community of fellow dreamers or join one that already exists: *www.AmazingDreamers.com.*

Life will rush in, systems will fall apart, and you may have meltdowns. Being a dreamer doesn't mean you won't have setbacks or ever be afraid. Quite the contrary. It's incredibly freeing to fail without considering yourself a failure or to be afraid and to risk anyway. Successful people have ups and downs and live to tell. By sharing your life's experiences and magical moments of fear and of courage, you can best serve the world.

In summary:

1. Separate your dreams from your fears.
2. Clearly recognize your doubts.
3. Identify if overcoming your obstacles will require beliefs or strategies.
4. Prove that you believe in your dream by taking action.
5. Learn the necessary skills or get assistance.
6. Talk to everyone you meet and make every conversation count.

Johnny Murillo has been a professional speaker for more than twenty years. He has traveled nationally and internationally, motivating thousands of people to make positive choices, start a new path, take the risks needed, and live life to the fullest.

He is the former co-host of *It's A New Day*, a morning radio talk show in Sacramento, CA. As an entrepreneur, film actor, ordained pastor, and radio personality, Johnny's insights are reflected in his presentations on how to become motivated, how to encourage your team to excel in business and community service, and how to become a Superhero Leader!

For more information or to contact Johnny, visit: *www.Johnnymurillo.com*, email him at *Johnny@Johnnymurillo.com*, or call 916-343-6074.

Chapter Nineteen

Are You a Superhero?

Johnny Murillo

I'll never forget that early Colorado September morning when my ten-year-old son came to my bedroom and woke me up with a concerned, confused look on his face. He gently nudged me out of my sleep saying, "Dad, there was an attack in New York."

I immediately knew he did not completely understand what he was saying, but the look of fear on his face sent me a signal that something bad had just happened. I jumped up from bed and went with him to see the news reports that were now on every channel. We both sat in silence as the second tower came down. We, like the rest of the world, were stunned to see such a world-changing catastrophe. The reports of the attack on the Pentagon and United Airlines flight 93 crashing in Pennsylvania were coming in. It was on that September 11th morning that I looked at my little boy and realized that we were witnessing an event that would change everything. His life would never be the same. The terrorists behind the attack had made a decision that would affect the future of my children and that of every American forever. It was a defining moment in all of our lives.

Heroism, Redefined

That day redefined heroism. Before that day we, as a society would look to athletes and entertainers as heroes. Our definition of heroism - post 9/11 – became quite different. I could still hear Todd Beamer's brave voice aboard UA flight 93 saying "Let's Roll," leading the charge of the first American attack of the new war on terrorism.

The picture of an emergency worker racing up the stairwell of the second tower is seared into my memory; he was heading into danger while civilians were running past him to safety. The facial expression of that New York firefighter expressed the heart of a true "Super hero."

From that day forward, our superheroes are now firefighters, police officers, EMTs, and our brave military. Their costumes are not capes and tights, but rather fire proof coats, bullet proof vests, and protective gloves. They fight evil not with X-ray vision and superpowers, but with night scopes and GPS technology. They wear helmets and gas masks, ready to serve and protect. National adversity redefined national heroism.

What about you? What Superhero costume is hanging in your closet? Do you remember the Hulk? He was one of my childhood heroes. During the day, he was a mild-mannered guy. But when something stirred him up, he would turn into a huge, green giant... ready to save the day. His purpose was stirred by his passion to make a difference. He couldn't just sit back and let things happen; when he saw injustice, he had to take action.

What are you passionate about? What stirs you? Could it be an indication of your purpose, showing where you should focus your energy? Our forefathers were fed up with overbearing taxes. Lincoln was stirred by the injustice of slavery. Martin Luther King campaigned for civil rights. When you discover your passion, your life will transformed. You will feel an increased sense of freedom in all that you do.

Purpose = Passion
My wife, Terry, always battled sickness. As a child, she missed countless days of school. Other kids would get a sore throat, but Terry would get strep. We met in college and during the two years we dated, there were many times that I attended banquets and social events alone because my college sweetheart was sick. Eight years into our marriage and thousands of dollars in medical bills later, her constant battle with sickness finally brought her to a point where it was interfering with our ability to live normal lives. I was speaking in Phoenix and

I started to pack for our travel to New Mexico for a weekend of seminars and training. She couldn't get out of bed, so we had to cancel our event.

That day she realized that she had had enough of being sick and she decided to study the human body to discover how it works. She read numerous books on health and nutrition, and gained an understanding what the body needed to function optimally. She is now a certified nutritionist who enjoys improved health herself, and has also helped countless others to free themselves from the burden of sickness. It angers her to see sick children and adults – people suffering with diabetes and cancers – especially when their behavior could make a difference.

When it comes to illness, she transforms into a superhero. Only unlike the Hulk, she is a health superhero. She found a way to convert her passion into purpose.

A Culture of Mentorship

Jack Welch, former CEO and author of *Winning*, transformed General Electric from a struggling appliance company into a mega corporation. He attributes that success to creating a culture of mentorship. He required his leaders to spend a majority of their efforts on developing those leaders directly beneath them. That is totally contrary to the cut-throat culture that many organizations seem to have. Even so, he took the risk and it paid off well. Now, many corporate leaders trace their roots back to the culture of mentorship as defined by Jack Welch.

At one point in my career, I was working with troubled teens in Denver. I had a passion to make a difference in the lives of these young people. That spring, one of the leaders in my industry, Wayne Cordeiro, a man whose books I had read and whose work I had followed, was speaking at a conference. He had a similar passion and a great organization that reached thousands of people. While attending the conference, I had a chance to meet him. We had such a great connection and continued to communicate over the weeks that followed. Within a month, he invited me into a mentorship relationship. He said that for one year, he would place me on his staff with a salary, and even help with my moving expenses. This was a dream come true!

The problem was that he lived in Hawaii, about 3,300 miles away from Denver, where I was working at the time. It would have been a tremendous life change for my family - leaving our home, my wife's family, my job. But the opportunity to be mentored by one of my heroes was the chance of a lifetime. So, we made the sacrifice and moved. For the next 12 months, my family "suffered" on the Island of Oahu, in the state of Hawaii, going to luaus, snorkeling, surfing, all while I was being mentored. Sharing this time with my mentor changed my life; it made me a better leader and now I am committed to mentoring.

Wayne Cordiero instilled a culture of mentorship within me as he has done with his organization. He inspires superhero leaders, people who are pursued by people who see something special in them. It's important to have a mentor and to be a mentor to others. Together, we are able to increase our effectiveness by influencing others to share our passion, to show them more effective ways to achieve their goals, and to provide support and encouragement. And, we need to find our own Superheroes, from whom we can learn and grow.

Everybody's Favorite Superhero: Superman
He was faster than a speeding bullet, stronger than a locomotive, able to leap tall buildings in a single bound! Superman, the leader of the Justice League, was born with incredible abilities.

But he had a weakness. No matter how strong or fast he was, whenever exposed to Kryptonite he would fall like a rag doll, helpless and defenseless in the hands of his enemies. Ask yourself, "What is MY Kryptonite?" Think about what brings you to the point of quitting or burning out.

We all have an emotional tank. If it's full, we are energized, creative, and ready to lead. If it's empty, we feel drained. If we don't bother to refill it, we may fall into a time of burn out and despair, or maybe even depression, leading to regrettable life changes.

You can't operate successfully on an empty tank. Here is the key to avoiding what I call "Kryptonite burnout." Determine what fills you and what drains you and balance them. Today, anybody can be a Superhero leader. The world is in need of Superhero leaders. Washington needs politicians who cannot be bought. Wall Street needs leaders who are not poisoned by greed. Main Street is in need of superhero citizens, and children are in need of Superhero parents!

Whether you are a CEO, a small business owner, or a great soccer mom, the chances are that you are already leading people. No matter what costume you have hanging in your closet, choose to be a superhero leader.

Brian Tracy has started, built, managed or turned around twenty-two businesses and has consulted for more than 1,000 businesses worldwide. He is president of Brian Tracy University of Sales and Entrepreneurship, a private, online college for business and entrepreneurship. He is also chairman and CEO of Brian Tracy International, a company specializing in the training and development of individuals and organizations.

He has written more than forty books on personal and business success that have been translated into thirty-four languages. He has written and produced more than 300 audio and video learning programs.

Brian speaks on the subjects of personal and professional development to corporate and public audiences, including the executives and staffs of many of America's largest corporations. His exciting talks and seminars on leadership, selling, self-esteem, goals, strategy, creativity and success psychology bring about immediate changes and long-term results. For more information, visit *www.BrianTracy.com* or call 858-436-7300.

Chapter Twenty

The Uncertainty Principle

Brian Tracy

The Law of Probabilities

Some people think that "luck" is a major factor in business success. In fact, people who are failures almost always attribute their lack of achievement to "bad luck." They say, "Successful people are simply those who have had a lucky break."

The fact is that, because of the mental laws that govern the human universe, there really is no such thing as luck. Everything happens for a reason, whether or not you know the reason. Instead of luck, there is the law of probabilities.

Probability theory, which is taught in the business faculties of most universities, dates back about 300 years. It says that there is a probability that everything will happen. There is a probability that an airplane will crash. There is a probability that you will live to be

100. There is a probability that you will become rich. All of finance, economics, business, life insurance, and science of every kind is based on the law of probabilities.

The Uncertainty Principle

The German physicist, Werner Heisenberg, won a Nobel Prize in Physics in 1932 for his breakthrough concept called Heisenberg's Uncertainty Principle.

This principle says that in any group of molecules, using probability theory, it is possible to predict that a certain percentage of those molecules will act in a certain way. His breakthrough, which led to his Nobel Prize, was his proof that you could never tell exactly *which* molecules they would be.

How does this apply to business and entrepreneurship? Of 100 people who start work at the age of 21, the following will be true by the time they reach the age of 65: five of them will be wealthy, 15 will be well off, and the other 80 percent will be dependent upon pensions or relatives, broke, still working, or dead. But the uncertainty principle tells us that we do not know exactly which ones will be in which category with the passing of time.

The good news is that you can *influence* the probabilities of something happening to you by thinking and acting in a specific way. For example, you can dramatically increase the probabilities that you will be successful and wealthy in business by doing certain things that have been proven to work over and over again until you get successful results. And it will not be a matter of luck.

Throughout my book, *The Way to Wealth,* I share proven principles that are practiced by every entrepreneur who has gone from rags to riches, from poverty to affluence, from frustration to the realization of his or her full potential. By applying these ideas every day in your business and financial life, you can dramatically increase the probabilities that you will become wealthy as a business owner.

Take Charge of Your Life

Perhaps the starting point of all success in business and personal life revolves around the acceptance of *responsibility.* This is a major issue that is continually debated, especially by people who blame their problems on their parents, their bosses, politics, society, or something else. There seems to be an irresistible tendency among unsuccessful people to see the reasons for their problems and difficulties as originating outside of themselves. They refuse to accept responsibility.

The fact is that you are 100 percent responsible for the person you are, what you are, and everything that happens to you. Your parents may be responsible for providing for you up to the age of 18, but after that you are on your own. You are responsible for everything that happens to you from that moment onward.

In almost every book, article, and study of success, the principle of personal responsibility emerges right at the beginning. The first chapter of Stephen Covey's bestselling book *The Seven Habits of Highly Effective People* is on personal responsibility. The first chapter of Jack Canfield's bestseller, *The Success Principles,* is on personal responsibility. Throughout the ages, the hallmark of leaders and all other superior people is that they accept an inordinately high degree of responsibility for themselves, their lives, the people around them, and everything that happens to them.

Refuse to Blame or Make Excuses

With regard to business, money, entrepreneurship, and careers, you become an "economic adult" only when you take charge of your own life and refuse to blame anyone or make excuses for anything. You move to full maturity when you begin to see yourself as the primary creative force in your own life.

Weak people, nonleaders, and those who suffer failure and frustration as adults, repeatedly condemn, complain about, and criticize other people. They make excuses rather than progress. They blame others for their problems rather than accept responsibility. Because of this, they have only a limited future.

The hallmark of the successful entrepreneur, the person who eventually becomes wealthy by building a profitable business, is that he or she accepts complete responsibility for himself or herself, his or her business, and everything that happens, good or bad. He or she may not be "at fault" when cheated or mistreated by other people or when his or her business occasionally gets into trouble, but this person accepts complete responsibility for his or her actions and for everything he or she does afterwards.

The mark of the mature person is his or her level of "response-ability." This is the ability to respond positively, constructively, and effectively to the inevitable difficulties and crises of adult life, especially business life. To be a successful entrepreneur and to launch yourself on the way to wealth, you must leave your excuses behind. You must accept complete responsibility for your choices and decisions, and for everything that happens as a result of them, from this day forward.

Marion Grobb Finkelstein is a communications specialist who delivers inspiring, entertaining and thought-provoking conference keynotes and a variety of communication-related training sessions. She lives in Ottawa, Canada. Marion works with corporate, government and non-profit organizations interested in improving their effectiveness through enhanced communication skills.

Marion has overseen national marketing campaigns, media issues, and award-winning cablevision shows. A member of the Canadian Association of Professional Speakers and the International Federation for Professional Speakers, Marion is an award-winning Toastmaster and has worked as Director of Communications at international airports, national museums and with federal institutions. She is True Colors™ and Personality Dimensions™ certified.

Improve communication skills for you or your team! Sign up for Marion's free "Communication Tips" e-newsletter. Visit Marion at *www.MarionSpeaks.com*, e-mail *Marion@MarionSpeaks.com*, or call 613-821-0600.

Chapter Twenty-One

Life's A Gamble

Marion Grobb Finkelstein

It was many years ago, as a kid, I heard my mom say something you've probably heard your mother or father say too. She told me, "Marion, the only sure thing in life is death and taxes. Apart from that, there are no guarantees." True enough, Mom. This thing we call "life" is a risky business. And it's worth the gamble.

When was the last time you took a risk, stepped out of your comfort zone, and experienced great uncertainty? Perhaps you're in a new job. Or maybe you're engaged to be married. Or you're trying an avant-garde medical procedure. In whatever direction your life is headed, it's your decisions, risks, and gambles that are leading you there.

Why Gambling on a Few Risks is a Good Thing
OK, let's face it. Some people are risk-averse to the nth degree. They don't like to gamble anything, ever. They enjoy certainty and plot

the future based rigidly on the past. They are uncomfortable with the unknown, and predictably go to university, get a secure job, start planning their retirement from their first day of employment, count on their 2.3 kids and know what retirement home they'd prefer.

The difficulty comes when these people are thrown an unexpected curve and have no idea how to handle it. They lose their jobs. Their car is wrecked in an accident. Their investments take a nosedive. And they have no coping skills to carry on.

We experience loss when we take risks. Along with that, we gain coping skills and this prepares us for the next hammering around the corner. It's not so daunting when we know we've handled other losses and can ably cope with whatever life rolls in our direction.

Taking a few measured gambles means we're not going to win them all. Things don't always turn out the way we hope or want, and (here's the news flash) that's just perfect! Oh, I can hear you now, "Perfect? But Marion, how can not getting what I want be perfect?" Well, let me explain. It's ideal because it's through failing and falling that we practice dusting ourselves off and moving forward. It builds resilience.

Gambling a bit also allows us to live in our "uncomfort zone." It stretches us past our normal boundaries and pulls us to grow in different directions. It's through this experience that we are nudged into new adventures we would otherwise miss.

How to Stack Life's Deck in Your Favor

A friend of mine has made his livelihood in leading edge, environment-friendly products. No sooner has he sold off one big company to an international buyer than he's involved with the launch of another. A gamble? You bet; but not a reckless one. He minimizes risk by getting his information straight. In short, he does his homework. You can too.

⊛   Ask questions

Knowing how to ask the right questions of the right people can help you make informed decisions and stack the deck in your favor. It can also shorten a steep and expensive learning curve.

What decisions are you grappling with? Chances are you already know someone who has wrestled through the same decision-making process that you're going through. He or she would probably be flattered and delighted to share some amazing insights with you. Ferret out the experts in the area in which you need knowledge. These people can help to guide you. Even if you pay to get this information and then decide not to proceed, it is money and time well spent. Consider educating yourself as "gambling insurance" so you can hedge your bets.

❀ Build on your experience

With every gamble you take, you learn. You discover what works, and perhaps more importantly, what doesn't. Your contact list grows as you broaden your circle with experts, coaches, and colleagues who form an ever-growing support team. As your knowledge, experience, and contacts grow, so too does your confidence. You are in a better position to take a gamble because you know that you have the skills to make informed choices, and regardless of the outcome, you'll be just fine. You have to start somewhere. Let that start be here and now.

❀ Know your comfort zone

When I was living in Reno, Nevada, after a long day in the office, a colleague and I decided to grab a bite and hit a few slots. He saw me cautiously feeding my hard earned cash into the hungry mouths of the machines. Maybe it was my lip-biting, fidgeting, or glassy-eyed stare at the one-armed bandit that tipped him off, but somehow he read that I was way out of my comfort zone. That's when he leaned over and told me something I will never forget. He said, "Never bet anything you're not prepared to lose". This bit of wisdom has since guided the gambles in life that I take ... or don't. It will guide you too.

An Acid Test That Will Help

If you're wondering whether or not you should take a gamble, here's an exercise that I've used quite successfully. Picture yourself years from now, in a home for seniors. Imagine you're at the stage in your life where more years are behind than before you. As you sit in your rocking chair thinking back at the moment when you had to decide to take that gamble, (the one you're now considering), do you rock a bit and think, "Whew, glad I dodged that bullet!" or... do you wish you had another chance to go for it? In other words, is this something that you will regret not doing 10, 20, 30 years down the road? Are you prepared to lose what you gamble? If so, it might be worth the risk.

Indecision is a Decision

You never know what life is going to deal you. Admittedly, it's a gamble to make decisions and take actions. Here's an interesting twist to consider -- it's also a gamble to do nothing. Indecision *is* a decision. For example, say you're struggling with the decision to cut or grow your hair. As you are mired in indecision, your hair continues growing. If you're deciding to stay in a job, a house, or a marriage, *your indecision is a decision*. And that decision is also a gamble.

What Separates Winners from Losers?

Even if you've gambled before and not gotten what you wanted, all is not lost if you got the message out of the mess. Let me repeat that – get the message out of the mess.

Did it hurt so deeply that you know you never want to gamble that much again? Or are you regretting the one that got away, the gamble that you turned your back on and have been kicking yourself over ever since? That's great! Don't beat yourself up. Instead, be glad that now you know more about yourself and your comfort zones. Then use that newly acquired knowledge.

Winners celebrate every step along the process, not just the end result. They enjoy every high and low of the journey and focus on what they've learned. They take time to reflect on how far they have come. They throw up their arms and enjoy the ride.

Winners understand that the roll of the dice is random. Sometimes you win, and sometimes -- unfairly and even though all logic would suggest otherwise -- you lose. Bad things just happen. Young people get diagnosed with arthritis. Parents get Alzheimer's. People lose businesses. Some of life is just luck of the draw. My eldest sister, Linda, has an expression that sums it up. She says, "It's not justice, it just is". Winners get that fact. They realize that life will deal them hands that aren't fair. It's not personal and it does not devalue them. It just is.

It was a gamble when Tim and Jenny decided to start their family. Jenny was quickly approaching her forties and painfully aware of the increased birth risks. Tim, perhaps in an effort to console his wife, swore that he was happy with or without children. As the years passed with still no children, the couple sought medical intervention. Four pregnancies later, still no kids. They pursued adoption, and after four years of waiting, not one match. Their life had unexpectedly been rewritten. They gambled, and to some, it appeared that they'd lost. But in true winner fashion, Tim and Jenny chose to focus on the wins. Jenny confided to her closest friends how grateful she was to have experienced pregnancy, realizing that not every woman is afforded this opportunity. Tim converted the savings they had put aside for children into early retirement and trips down south for him and his wife. Tim and Jenny are winners.

A Final Thought

Years ago, my mom told me there were no guarantees in life. That truism lives on today. Life really is a gamble ... so roll the dice and let the games begin!

Ten Evaluation Points to
Determine if Becoming a Coauthor in
The Power of the Platform
is Right for You

If you are a professional speaker, an esteemed Toastmaster, a business professional or an author who has a special message to share, here are ten evaluation points to determine if you would like to become a coauthor in an upcoming edition of The Las Vegas Convention Speakers Bureau's *Power of the Platform* series of books.

The world of professional speaking is a highly competitive industry. I meet many professional speakers who have never published a book; they have no way to share their message with their audiences once they've finished speaking other than with handouts, which – in many cases – quickly get discarded.

Many of the people I meet tell me that they are working on a book. When asked what it is about or how it is coming along, they point to their heads or hearts and say, "It's all right here...!" It's such a tragedy that they have an important message to share but don't know how to go about writing or publishing their story. Millions of people want to write a book; most have the ability and some have the drive, but few have the know-how.

Contributing to an anthology is the fastest, easiest, and most affordable way to become published. Here is my promise to you. After you evaluate these ten points, you will know – without a shadow of a doubt – if this project is for you.

That being said, here are ten points to evaluate to determine if becoming a coauthor in the Las Vegas Convention Speakers Bureau's *Power of the Platform* book series is right for you:

1. Celebrity Status. Let's face it; we live in a society that is obsessed with celebrities. People look at you and treat you differently when you are a published expert; you'll have instant "Celebrity Status."

2. Massive Exposure. Each *Power of the Platform* goes out to at least twenty coauthors the day it is printed. Each coauthor then shares these books with their audiences all over the world. Add to that traditional distribution, and your book will reach an audience more than ten times greater than if you were to produce it yourself – with or without a publisher. Plus, as President of the Las Vegas Convention Speakers Bureau, I will personally put these books in the hands of meeting planners everywhere. That could mean more *paid speaking engagements* for you! Add Internet support and you will become a part of a publishing phenomenon.

3. Power of Associations. Perhaps the masses have not heard of you or me, but they know the international speakers, writers, and television and film stars like Jack Canfield, Brian Tracy, and Les Brown. When people see that you are a coauthor in a book with these personal development celebrities, they will associate you with them.

4. Credibility. Once you become a published author, you become an expert in the minds of people. Combine this with the power of association and your credibility is established instantly. Who would not want to do business with you?

5. Business Card on Steroids. People throw away business cards and brochures no matter how fancy they are, but they will not throw away a book! They will keep that book, read it and re-read it. Your information is right there in front of them all the time. Talk about a business card with power!

6. The Power of a Great First Impression. How many of your competitors are sending out media kits with a book that they co-authored with nationally recognized experts?

7. Easy to get published. We make this process so easy a child could do it. There are two ways to do this. You write your story which we will professionally edit or we will ghost write the entire chapter for you. It doesn't get easier than that!

8. Profit Center. You will have a product that will earn you more than 70% profit per book. Our books are the highest quality and the content is vital. The investment is minor but the rewards are unlimited. PLUS, you will receive an *e-book version* of your book which you can sell as a download...no additional cost to you, but profits galore!

9. Increased Business. Just ONE paid speaking engagement because an event or meeting planner read your chapter and you're ahead of the game! If you are a speaker, a consultant, or an entrepreneur, this book will give your business a tremendous boost. There will also be a companion audio book and the potential to speak at an upcoming *Power of the Platform* seminar!

10. We pay all the publishing costs. As a publisher, we pay for all the professional editing, formatting, book cover design, marketing campaigns and printing of the books. Currently, the only requirement you have as a coauthor is to purchase 500 books at the discount price of $6.72 per book. The book retails for $19.95, and your profit is $13.23 per book. We also supply you with a professional press release and sales aids to help you market and sell your books. This is a team venture.

Let me ask you, *"Do you believe that gaining massive exposure to a targeted market and leveraging yourself in a position that your competitors cannot touch could help explode your business, income and profits?"* If you answered yes, then being a co-author in *The Power of the Platform* book series is right for you. Top this off with the fact that this type of dynamic marketing doesn't cost you, but rather *pays you* from the profits you earn selling your books and you'll agree - it just doesn't get any better than this!

We look forward to helping you achieve your greatest success.

Robin Jay

President, Las Vegas Convention Speakers Bureau

www.LVCSB.com

Call us today at (702)460-1420 to see if there are any spots still available in our upcoming book. In a matter of weeks, you could be a featured coauthor in the next

***Power of the Platform* book. Call me right now!**

The Las Vegas Convention Speakers Bureau
provides professional keynote, motivational,
and inspirational speakers and entertainers for
conventions, conferences, seminars and meetings.

*Whether you need a speaker to improve your
company's attitude, to boost productivity and
sales, or to share the latest insights on networking,
leadership, communication, customer service,
humor, management, branding, business or
diversity, the Las Vegas Convention Speakers
Bureau has just the right speaker to make your
meeting the most memorable, ever!*

*We will work with you one-on-one to determine
your special needs, and then recommend only the
finest, most appropriate and engaging speakers or
entertainers – each of whom will work passionately
to deliver impact to your event, conference or
convention.*

*For a presentation that will be the highlight of
your event, please call or e-mail us immediately!
We look forward to working with you to create an
event that will net high scores for your keynotes,
breakouts, and general sessions.*

LAS VEGAS
CONVENTION
SPEAKERS BUREAU
~ Featuring World-Class Speakers,
Entertainers & Athletes
Robin@LVCSB.com
www.LVCSB.com
702-460-1420

The Power of the Platform
Speakers on Success

If you would like to order additional copies of
The Power of the Platform: *Speakers on Success*
please visit our website at
www.ThePowerofthePlatform.com
or call 702-460-1420.

Special discounts are available on orders of
fifty books or more.

About the
The Las Vegas Convention Speakers Bureau
www.LVCSB.com

If you are a speaker and would like more
information on being listed with the Las Vegas
Convention Speakers Bureau or in being a featured
speaker in an upcoming edition of *The Power of the
Platform,* please contact us immediately.
E-mail: *Robin@LVCSB.com*
or call 702-460-1420.

*Engage your passion ~ Do what you love, help
others, and make money!*

*The Las Vegas Convention Speakers Bureau
also offers coaching on speaking, writing,
publishing, and marketing. We have a team of
experts and the resources to help you achieve
all of your speaking and publishing goals.*